EXECUTE
YOUR
VISION

EXECUTE YOUR VISION

The Practical Art
of Ministry Leadership

Bill Easum
Scott Musselman

Abingdon Press™
Nashville

EXECUTE YOUR VISION:
THE PRACTICAL ART OF MINISTRY LEADERSHIP

Copyright © 2016 by Bill Easum and Scott Musselman

All rights reserved.

This book is printed on acid-free paper.

Library of Congress Cataloging-in-Publication Data has been requested.

ISBN: 978-1-5018-1899-8

Scripture quotations unless noted otherwise are from the Common English Bible. Copyright © 2011 by the Common English Bible. All rights reserved. Used by permission. www.Com monEnglishBible.com.

Scripture quotations from The Authorized (King James) Version. Rights in the Authorized Version in the United Kingdom are vested in the Crown. Reproduced by permission of the Crown's patentee, Cambridge University Press.

16 17 18 19 20 21 22 23 24 25—10 9 8 7 6 5 4 3 2 1
MANUFACTURED IN THE UNITED STATES OF AMERICA

Contents

Introduction:
Executing Your Vision

After that I will pour out my spirit upon everyone; / your sons and your daughters will prophesy, / your old men will dream dreams, / and your young men will see visions. (Joel 2:28)

Dreams and visions are amazing gifts from God. They are at the heart of God's plan for our lives. Anyone can have an idea, but not everyone will experience that vision come to fruition. This book explores how to turn visions into reality in a fast-moving world that is changing at an exponential rate.

A lot of books have been written the past few decades on how to lead in a rapidly changing world. So why should you read another one? That question deserves an answer.

While most church books on navigating change deal with tactics like my (BE) book, *Unfreezing Moves*, this book focuses on the obstacles that keep most leaders from turning their visions into reality.[1] *(Note: Specific references in this book by Bill Easum will be notated as BE; those by Scott Musselman will be SM.)*

It takes leadership for a vision to come into being. Before going any further, let's define how we use the terms *leadership* and *leaders*. *Leadership* is the art of helping others achieve their potential. *Leaders* don't coerce someone to do their will; instead they invite them to join them on a journey of turning a vision into reality. A wonderful metaphor for leadership is that of a spiritual midwife. As a midwife assists parents in the birth of their child, leaders assist others in the birth of their God-given gifts. For more on this, see my (BE) book, *Leadership on the Other Side.*[2]

In consulting with over 700 churches in the past twenty-five years, one problem clearly stands out above all the rest. Pastors find it hard to execute a vision. Ideas aren't hard to come by; making them happen is another thing altogether.

This book will note how the church missed out on prime opportunities during the middle of the twentieth century in the United States when our culture went through a significant transition. Pastors, especially those who are younger, would do well to learn from these past lessons and apply that to a similar moment of transition in our contemporary society. If you have any comments about concepts in the book and how you experience them in your particular setting, we would love to engage you in conversation. Just send us an e-mail at this address: http://effectivechurch.com/contact/.

As you read, you will find Reflection Points. Take time to actually do the exercises. We know the tendency is to ignore such pieces and continue reading. Don't shortchange yourself. Do the exercises. They will help you apply the concepts to your situation.

So read away and put one word on your refrigerator—FOCUS.

The Key to Everything

We live in a time when it is easy for a dream to become a nightmare. Why is that so? Because we're living in a world where most things that will be important over the next twenty years have not yet been invented.

Few thinking individuals would deny that we're living in a time of radical change. We describe it as one of "radical discontinuity." But no matter what we call it, our world is going through a seismic shift of epic proportions, which makes it even harder to turn a vision into reality.

I (BE) first wrote about this upheaval in my book, *Dancing with Dinosaurs*, where I noted the "crack in history" into which the old world is disappearing, leaving us in a constantly changing world without any rules.[1] Even though the book became a bestseller, and all but one of the predictions came true, few leaders adapted to the new world that I described. That begs the question: "Why do so many churches continue to minister as if nothing has changed?"

The church is burying its head in ostrich-like fashion because even though people know something is happening to their way of life, they haven't fully embraced it. They know it in their head but not in their heart. They are like the people who are told by the doctor they are so overweight that if they don't do something about it they will die. Yet they still go out and eat a big bag of french fries. That kind of behavior is deadly, and that is what is happening in the church today.

So what's a leader who is aware that something radically different is happening in the world and wants to help the church grow to do? To respond to this question, let's explore THE KEY TO EVERYTHING.

The One Key That Unlocks Everything

There is one key that must be addressed before the average leader and/or church can thrive. This concept is so pervasive to all of life that every chapter in this book will come back to it.

The key to everything is to fully embrace the reality and implications that we are living through only the fourth major transition in all of Western civilization. When people internalize this fact, they will be more open to trying new ideas.

On the surface, this key may not seem so monumentally important. But we assure you it is at the heart of why 85 percent of all churches in the United States are in decline. They do not or will not come to grips with the fact that everything is undergoing change (except, of course, the Gospel) and are not willing to turn their thinking upside-down.

Too many people have a limited knowledge of history, so they don't understand the implications of this transition. You know the old saying, "Those who don't know history are doomed to repeat it." Well, that is what is happening today. What we are experiencing is nothing new to history. It has been played out three times before, and each time everything—and we do mean everything—changed. Everything and everyone needed to adapt, or they became obsolete.

What the Past Tells Us about the Future

Until now, there have only been three major transitions in all of Western culture. Pause to think about that statement a moment. In all of our recorded history, there have been only three significant transitions for how we understand society. But those three tell us something profound about how to address the incredible changes we experience today.

Take a look at the following chart.

First Transition	Second Transition	Third Transition	Fourth Transition
400 CE End of Classical Age	1400 CE End of Middle Ages	1954 CE End of Modern Age	2000 CE End of Post-modern Age
Length of Age	Length of Age	Length of Age	Length of Age
1000 years	550 years	50 years	—

If you are following the chart, something significant should jump out at you.

Reflection: Before reading further, write down the meaning of this chart for you and your church. Analyze the chart, and make a list of its implications. You will need this list to refer back to later. Please don't look at the next paragraph until you do this.

The first big thing you should notice is the rate of change. The time between transitions is decreasing dramatically. The length of the Modern Age was half that of the Middle Ages. The Postmodern Age was one-tenth as long as the Modern Age. Change in our definitive cultural expressions is escalating at an exponential rate.

Based on this rate of change, the second thing that should jump out at you is that it is quite possible we will experience another major transition within the next ten years. Could we have two major transitions in twenty or thirty years when there have only been three before? What does this say to our heritage of charting our culture's journey through a period of time we label an *age*? Can ten years even constitute an *age*? If you need further data to prove this point, consider the following.

To reach an audience of fifty million, it took:

- Radio—38 years.
- TV—13 years.
- Internet—4 years.
- iPod—3 years.
- Facebook—2 years.

What's next?

We can only conclude that everything is speeding up. The faster an organization can adapt to change, the more likely it is to turn its vision into reality. When the rate of change in an organization is slower than the world around it, that organization is in trouble.

In "Billionaires on a Mission: Titans at the Table with Betty Liu" featuring Bill Gates and Mike Bloomberg, Bloomberg said something that all churches should ponder. He said, "In the next two or three years, we will improve technology more than it was done from the beginning of inventing electricity till today." [2] What is the impact of this for leadership?

4

When it comes to education, it means that printed content is significantly losing relevance. Flat screens with flat people won't be relevant much longer, opening the door for everything holographic.

When it comes to worship, it means that if a church can't transform its worship setting on a regular basis, it is no longer relevant to any person less than twenty years of age.

When it comes to communication, it means that there has to be a marriage of sights, sounds, and words in a seamless fashion if one wants to get the point across. Just telling a good story will no longer be enough.

For board meetings, it means that sitting at a table looking at a spreadsheet will no longer capture the imagination of upcoming generations. They will have to see 3-D graphs showing what the information is actually indicating and what the organization needs to do to capture the future.

Reflection: What thoughts come to mind as you ponder the influence of these statements on the quality and relevancy of your leadership?

Take a Second Look

First Transition	Second Transition	Third Transition	Fourth Transition
Polytheism	Monotheism	Denomina-tionalism	Agnosticism/ Tolerance
Oral tradition	Printing press	Newspapers	Digital

Let's examine some of the major issues that occurred at each transition. These have a more direct bearing on the church.

Reflection: Before reading further, write down your thoughts about what these changes mean to your ministry.

The first tier indicates we are now living in a time of anti-religion. This means several things:

- Clergy are no longer the most respected group.
- Pastors have to earn the trust of the public.
- Infant baptisms are going away.
- Denominations will continue to decline.
- Church weddings are giving way to civil ceremonies.

Very few people come to church on their own; the church has to go to them.

Here are some implications from the second tier of changes:

- Printed newsletters are ineffective.
- The church website, Facebook, Twitter, and Google are the portals of entry for most new people at your church.
- More people are worshipping online.
- Online giving is replacing the passing of the offering plate.
- Worship is becoming digital.
- Sunday school curriculum is becoming more like Vacation Bible School and *Veggie Tales*.

We're sure you can think of more, but you get the picture.

There are two huge implications.

First, place no longer matters. This is the basis for the multi-site revolution, which could become the norm by the midpoint of the century. Online worship will be even more pronounced, and small group ministries that meet in homes will be essential.

Second, the United States is the third largest mission field in the world, making it obvious why we need backyard missionaries.

Two metaphors best describe the discontinuity of our times—the national park and the jungle. The national park is a metaphor for pre1950s culture. The jungle is the emerging new world of the fourth transition. Let your imagination run wild thinking about the implications of moving from the national park to the jungle. If you want to see the full picture, read the book I (BE) wrote with Bill Tenny-Brittian, *Doing Ministry in Hard Times*.[3]

Reflection: Let your mind run wild with these two metaphors, and you will begin to understand the radical changes taking place in our culture.

I (BE) first rolled out these epic transitions and their implications in the fall of 2013 at a retreat for a few of the people I was coaching. As we discussed the transitions and the fact that there could be more in the next few decades, one person in the group said, "I think we've already entered the next transition—the Internet is changing everything."

Of course, it is too soon to tell whether this is the next transition or just a refinement of the current age, but observing the impact of the Internet on just about everything we do suggests we may already have entered the next transition.

7

Jumping the Curve

Most effective organizations understand one vital thing: you don't wait until something is broken before you fix it. While our natural instincts are to wait until the gradual changes reach a crisis and we have to act, organizations should take action before it is needed.

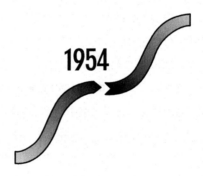

This action is called "jumping the curve," as discussed in the book, *Jumping the Curve: Innovation and Strategic Choice in an Age of Transition* by Nicholas Imparato and Oren Harari.[4] The object of jumping the curve is to institute change before it is needed. This requires leaders to keep good metrics on important facets of the organization and monitor them monthly. Before any kind of leveling off is experienced, a new way of action should already be in the pipeline. Anticipating the rate of change is one of the hallmarks of a good organization. That's why intuition is one of the essential qualities of great leaders—more on that later.

Consider the decline of Protestantism in the United States, which began in the mid-1960s. Very few people talked about it seriously until the 1990s. By then, it was too late to jump the curve since there was no curve to jump, only a dramatic downhill spiral with little chance of return. Leaders who understood history would know that the time to jump the curve was the late 1950s. They should have seen it coming. Why?

Notice what happened at the midpoint of 1954. That year, Bill Haley & His Comets unleashed what would become the first commercially successful rock-and-roll hit—"Rock Around the Clock."

The recording marked a cultural shift and the beginning of the end of a way of life. It caused polite society to blush in anger and teenagers to dance with glee. Even though there would be a profound effect on Christianity, the shift went virtually unnoticed by most church leaders. Those few who did take notice did their best to squash it and denounced it as evil or just a fad. It wasn't long before Woodstock, the Jesus movement, the space program, and Haight-Ashbury burst on the scene. In 1953, IBM introduced the first mass-produced computer, and in 1968, Hewlett Packard began marketing the personal computer. As Bob Dylan kept reminding us, "The times they are a-changin'." [5]

That very same decade, mainline denominations were enjoying the zenith of their prime without a hint of what was to happen to them in less than ten years. Few, if any, were aware that their dream was about to become a nightmare of declining numbers and perceived irrelevancy.

Meanwhile, in Benton, Arkansas, Sam Walton was experimenting with ways to outsell his competitors by offering lower prices. Over the next four decades, the store that became known as Wal-Mart replaced the neighborhood grocery store as well as any other store that carried what Wal-Mart sold. The landscape of many rural and urban areas was changed. Bigger was better. The rise of the megachurch got underway. Yet during that same period of time, denominations were pushing the importance of the neighborhood church as if the world was still running on 1950s time. In hindsight, such action is difficult to understand, but anyone keeping tabs on what was happening should have known something radically new was underway.

Reflection: What are the metrics you need to track in your church in order to jump the curve?

A New Way of Seeing Things

The farther we go through transition, the more important it will be for us to begin developing new ways of seeing old things. If the most important things for moving ahead in living life have not yet been invented, and we believe that is true, we will need to change our perspective on just about everything, except Jesus, of course.

But what does it mean to develop a new way of seeing old things? Let's answer this question by asking another question. What was the job of the Union Pacific Railroad? Was it the train business or the transportation business? If you answered "train business" and you were the CEO of Union Pacific, you would miss out on the opportunity of a lifetime—to get in early on the emerging new forms of transportation. If you answered "transportation," then you would have opened yourself to explore all forms of developing transportation, including automobiles, air travel, and even space travel.

Now apply that to the church. When you think of worship, what do you think of—traditional or contemporary? If you answered with either one, you are seeing things as they are now rather than how they will be.

A better answer would be "neither." Opting for style is nothing more than being in the "train business." Style isn't what worship is about. Worship is about connecting God and people. Focusing on style is why we have worship wars. It is why so many churches are missing out on the greatest opportunity of a lifetime—creating the package of worship to fit the transition without altering the Gospel. This is the most important change in our lifetime, but most will fail to make it because they are focused on their preferred style of worship rather than effectively transmitting the message.

If we are going to go through more major transitions in the near future, then we haven't yet seen the style of worship that will ultimately emerge. But if we see worship as connecting people with God, instead of traditional or contemporary, we have a better chance of being able to see and implement the next needed form of worship.

The bottom line is this: to see old things in new ways, we have to get *self* out of the way and replace it with the kingdom. Once personal opinions and preferences are removed, we can consider the situation from a fresh perspective.

The Importance of Intuition

Twenty years ago, I (SM) was a pastor in a large church. We had great programming and a prestigious reputation in the region. However, as I looked around, I didn't see lives being transformed through a spiritual journey with Jesus. Church attendance was declining, but we still had lots of people and money.

I prayed (be careful what you pray for) that God would place me in a church that would make a difference in people's lives. I ended up with a wonderful church where people were willing to experiment with methodology. The goal was simple—pursue what God's church looks like for the twenty-first century.

In our consulting, we often run into church people who appear bewildered with their church's state of affairs. They don't have a clue why their church is now rapidly declining. Welcome to the reality for 85 percent of the churches in the United States.

As stated earlier, we are living in a time of transition from the national park to the jungle. National parks seldom change. They are safe places as long as you follow the rules, and there are lots of rules. However, we now have been thrust into a world best described as a jungle. If you've ever been in a jungle, you know it is not a safe place. It has only one rule, the survival of the fittest. That's the world we live in today.

In a world that can best be described as a jungle, one trait rises to the top—intuition.

Intuition is the most important skill of a leader in the jungle because no one knows for sure what lies around the corner. Since the terrorist attacks of September 11, 2001, and the economic downfall of 2008, no one feels safe or sure about what's coming next. That is the primary difference between the world many of us were born into and the one we are called to minister in today. Such a world requires blazing new trails and taking enormous risks. The only way one can take such risks is by relying on intuition.

Someone asked me (BE) if intuition could be learned. My answer surprised the person. "Yes," I responded. I then told the person about a conversation I had with two scientists at a fishing village at the edge of the Darien jungle on the border of Panama and Columbia, two hundred miles from any road, phone lines, or electricity. I had a day off from fishing when these two scientists emerged at our camp after spending two weeks in the jungle studying bugs. They looked and smelled awful.

After they'd cleaned up, we visited over dinner and discussed their trip. When I asked what the most important thing to know about the jungle was, their response was immediate: "The jungle is never the same from day to day. It changes overnight." That led me to ask, "How do you know where to go?" They replied, "Of course we have a compass (GPS doesn't work in the jungle), but when we come to what we might call a fork in the road and need to decide which way to go, that's where intuition comes in. The more you travel the jungle, the easier it is to be intuitive about what lies around the corner."

Then I asked, "What about the compass?" They said, "Remember that the jungle changes every hour. Make a trail today, and it's gone next week. So even though you have a compass that is fairly accurate, it always needs to be verified. You still have to make some calculated guesses about which way to go to avoid an impasse."

After our conversation, I began to think about my ministry over the years. I was surprised to see the similarities today between ministry and the jungle. When I started out, the national park was a world of probabilities. Today, the jungle is a world of wild cards that mess up every well-conceived plan. How is one to lead in such a world? Intuition is what allows us to see old things in new ways.

So if intuition is the most needed skill in the jungle, how do we develop or improve our intuition? Remember what the scientist said: "The more you travel in the jungle, the easier it is to be intuitive about what lies around the corner." This is why we tell pastors to spend less time with churched folks and to spend more time with unchurched young adults—the jungle people.

Reflection: When was the last time you intentionally spent time away from churched people to get a sense of the emerging new world?

The following are some ways to spend time in the jungle:

- Spend at least one-half of your time with unconnected people out in the community. There is an old saying that after a person has been in the church three years, they don't know any non-Christians anymore. The same is true with pastors. If you want to know how to traverse the new world, you need to spend more time with non-Christians than you spend with Christians. Using demographic studies can help you understand who is in your community. But while these studies can help, they never take the place of getting to know your community firsthand. I (BE) spent every Friday night for eight years at a bar called the Fractured Fox listening to the stories of people who were either trying to cling to life or running from it.

- Read books in several fields outside the realm of religion. This will give you a perspective you would never get in the office and helps you come to more "aha" moments.

14

- Work around the edges of your religious group (denomination, association, or network). You will never find the status quo at the edge, nor will you hear "we've never done it that way before." Maximize the edges by attending events beyond those put on by your denomination, networking with pastors in other traditions, talking with young people, or visiting new websites.

- Watch sitcoms even if it kills you. Knowing and understanding what people are watching gives you insight into the jungle and helps develop your intuition.

- Challenge yourself to dream beyond that which you think you are capable because this is where you meet intuition.

- Embrace risk and don't be afraid of mistakes. There is power in a big failure if you are looking for the lessons. Always ask, "What am I learning from this experience that will help me see the future more clearly?" One of the things the scientists said was "Sometimes we have to make multiple attempts before we find a path that doesn't wind up at an impasse, and we have to backtrack."

- In times of great change, realize that whatever works well today is the seedbed for tomorrow's failure. As soon as you perfect what you are doing, move on to something else. Don't hang on too long to something that works well. Keep looking for ways to improve what you're doing—or do different things altogether.

- Trust your gut, not your critics. The first twenty years of my ministry, I (BE) received a lot of criticism from all fronts. I was told I was doing everything all wrong. Yet my congregation was growing faster than most churches in my tribe. I felt in my heart that what I was doing was right, but surely my peers couldn't all be wrong. There was a short period of time when I listened to them too much. It caused me to waste some of my earliest years. However, it soon became clear that what I was doing was leading my church to grow, and what they were advocating was resulting in the decline of their churches. So I began to follow my gut and tuned them out. You can do this if you are training yourself to listen to the hopes and dreams of the jungle.

- Of course, all the above is in vain if you aren't augmenting it with a heavy dose of the Holy Spirit. Listening to this still small voice is imperative if you are going to read the signs of the times. I (SM) am often reminded of the age-old translation of Proverbs 29:18, which is "When there is no vision, the people perish" (KJV). When I attended seminary, I was appalled at the lack of spiritual discipline exhibited by so many students and faculty. While this book is focused on what to do with a vision, we assume that you are finding the time to faithfully follow a spiritual journey that gives rise to such visions. At the congregation where I am a pastor, we have a membership covenant about how we will be a church that is based on the "one-another" verses of the Bible (where we are called to do such things as love, accept, and serve one another). We find our foundation for vision through prayer, reading the Bible, and spiritual conversations. Using this method, your intuition will be driven by God rather than by others or even your own personal preferences.

- If you're faced with a choice while training your intuition, don't blink, trust your gut, and take a leap. Consider this. How did Mark Zuckerberg know it was worth the time and money to develop Facebook? He didn't, but he understood the signs of the times. He knew people were craving interaction with other people. So he took a huge risk, and look what happened.

What is God calling you to do with your life? You are in a better position to take the necessary leap of faith if you are training your intuition to be like the biblical men of Issachar than if you are surrounding yourself with people who represent the national park perspective. You might want to put this scripture where you can't miss seeing it: "All these men understood the signs of the times and knew the best course for Israel to take" (1 Chr 12:32, author's paraphrase).

Radical Changes Are Needed

What happened every time an epic transition took place? Everything changed; nothing remained the same. Not only that; it changed at an even more rapid pace than in the past.

So why is this understanding of change the key to everything? It is because most church people will not buy into what appear to be crazy new ideas until they thoroughly understand the world in which they are living. People must internalize that everything they have worked for will go down the drain unless they make radical changes. It's that simple.

It's a well-known fact that people change in direct proportion to their discontent. Raise their discontent, and openness to change increases. The more people internalize that everything is turning upside-down, the more they are threatened, and the more they will change.

In case you're not yet convinced to change how you lead, take a look at the following facts from *Did You Know 3.0*:[6]

- Ten of the most in-demand jobs in 2010 didn't exist in 2004.
- There are over one billion people active monthly on Facebook.
- There are 50 million tweets a day.
- The first text was sent in 1992; today, the number of texts is more than the total population of the planet.
- There were 1,000 Internet devices in 1984; there were 1,000,000 in 1992; there were 1,000,000,000 in 2008.

- Half of what a first year college student learns this year will be out of date by their third year.
- 72 percent of Apple's source of income didn't exist five years ago.

If those statistics don't cause you to pause and think, nothing will. If there is to be any hope, we will have to make a leap of faith into a strange new way of thinking and acting. Don't look for stability, predictability, and order. Instead, embrace disequilibrium, and feel fortunate to live in such a time as this. Relish opportunity. Say to the challenges—BRING IT ON!

Reflection: Has this chapter opened your eyes to any blind spots in the way you think or act? Write them down before continuing.

Chapter Two
The Art of Execution

Many books have been written in the last decade on the importance of developing mission, vision, and value statements. Nothing is wrong with that. In fact, this is where all great work begins.

The problem is these actions will not turn vision into reality. It is one thing to cast a big, audacious, hairy goal. It is another to make it happen. There is a huge gap between vision and results. It's not the vision that grows a church. It's making the vision happen that grows a church. So what is the missing piece, especially when things are changing so rapidly?

Execution is the answer. Execution is what turns vision into reality. Yet very few leaders know how to help their staff implement the vision. Here's a truism that you can ignore at your own peril:

> Every manager isn't a leader, but every leader is a manager. If you can't manage (execute) the vision, you aren't a leader.

The Achilles' heel of the vast majority of pastors is their inability to manage. Even if they have a vision, they can't communicate what is necessary to make it a reality. They are unable to put a strategy together that brings their vision to fruition. Most often this happens because they are too busy giving pastoral care, but

19

that isn't even supposed to be part of a pastor's duties. Such care comes from within the congregation. Just read Acts 6 or Ephesians 4. Still, most churches expect their pastors to give pastoral care. The more pastoral support a pastor gives, the more likely the church is to decline.

Let's look at two examples of vision not coming to fruition.

Example One: In the middle of the night, Pastor Harry had a wonderful vision. He arrived all pumped up at the church office the next morning for the staff meeting. Harry began the meeting with the exclamation "God has shown me how to triple the number of disciples who worship here." He then went on to describe this vision in such detail that his staff could actually see the faces of the new people who would soon fill the building.

They discussed the details of the vision and the joy it could bring to their church and the kingdom. Then Harry said to the staff, "Go make it happen. If you have problems, come see me."

A year later, the church had not grown but dwindled in size. Harry and the staff couldn't understand why the vision had not become reality. The vision was so good and clear. It should have happened. But it didn't.

Example Two: About a decade or more ago, I (BE) worked with a pastor who was relocating his church. He took me out to the spot of land and walked me through it. He described in vivid detail each of the buildings and what would take place in them. He did it so magnificently I actually could see the buildings and the people worshipping and being discipled. A decade later, the number of people worshipping at that church remained virtually the same as it was at the old location, and the church began selling off some of the land to pay the bills.

20

|||||||||||||||||||||||||||||||||||||||||||||||||||||||||||||||||||||||||||||||||||||||||||||||||||||||||||||||||||||||

Reflection: Why do you think these two visions never materialized? What should the pastor have done differently? Write down your thoughts and compare them with what follows. Don't look ahead. That will spoil your learning experience.

|||||||||||||||||||||||||||||||||||||||||||||||||||||||||||||||||||||||||||||||||||||||||||||||||||||||||||||||||||||||

What Is Execution?

Execution is taking big visions and turning them into results. Execution is a systematic process of tenaciously discussing and sharing clear expectations, setting crisp goals and milestones, and then helping staff decide when and how things should get done and who is doing them, following through to ensure the vision is actually happening by being available for coaching and encouragement.

Whew! That's a mouthful, so let's take a look at each of these elements in the context of the two examples above.

Sharing Clear Expectations

In both cases, the vision was laid out. So you might think that everyone understands the expectations, right? Wrong. A vision can be identified, yet no one has a clue what you expect them to do to achieve that dream. Both pastors failed to make absolutely clear what each staff person's responsibility was in making the vision a reality.

It is amazing how many pastors and/or committees hire people without plainly indicating they expect the new person to grow the area for which they will be responsible. It amazes us that the

21

majority of staff we have surveyed feels that the growth of the church is the lead pastor's sole responsibility.

The lead pastor must make it clear that he or she expects each one of the staff to take responsibility for the growth of their area and help them decide how they will make that growth happen. The expectation is that all staff members grow their areas for overall church growth.

On my (BE) initial Sunday in the restart church where I spent twenty-four years, I told the personnel committee that the first year the church didn't grow I would resign. That is an example of setting out what you expect to happen. It was then up to me to ensure that growth occurred. I expected the church to grow. In fact, I was betting my entire ministry on it. When I began hiring, I stated that growth in their area was a requirement for tenure. My job was to coach and get them the training and resources they needed to make the vision come to fruition.

Now, you might think this expectation only applies to program staff. Not so. It should apply to everyone on the staff from the custodian to the office personnel. For instance, there was one church where the chief custodian was responsible for a large prison ministry. In another church of over two thousand people, there was only one person in the office. Her job was not to do all the work, but it was to train retired and stay-at-home parents to do the tasks. We're not suggesting you attempt either of these. We're just making the point that, in a thriving church, everyone on the staff should be able to see how their part—no matter how small—fits in and is vital to the overall growth of the church.

Setting Crisp Goals and Milestones

Here is a sample of what we normally see in a church's list of goals:

- Grow the youth program.
- Begin a visioning process.
- Add staff as needed.
- Increase the budget.

These are not goals; they're wishes. They can't be measured. So the odds are they will never happen. Instead, goals are needed that are Specific, Measurable, Achievable, Results-Focused, and Timely (S.M.A.R.T.).[1]

So here's an example of a crisp goal, or as some call it, a S.M.A.R.T. goal.

By next January, grow the youth attendance by 100 percent using youth worship on Sunday and small groups that create new servant leaders.

When setting goals, make sure you set two of them—a base goal and a stretch goal. The base goal is the actual target to which you hold the staff person accountable. The stretch goal is going beyond what is considered possible under normal circumstances. Stretch goals can't be achieved by incremental or small improvements but require extending oneself to the limit. The purpose of a stretch goal is to discover the actual limits of the person's potential.

You never know what is impossible until you try to go beyond what is viewed as possible. You will never discover the capabilities of a person if you set the goal too low. You always want to set the stretch goal just beyond what you feel someone is capable of achieving. Of course, you should remember that this is a stretch goal when it comes time to evaluate performance. It should lead to the uplifting of the human spirit. It should be a goal that inspires those doing the work and delights those for whom the work is done. It is the kind of goal that is key to staying ahead of our ever-changing world. Stretch goals will be hard to fulfill, but they're essential for our health and prosperity.

An example of a stretch goal is when Ed Young, pastor of Fellowship Church in Grapevine, Texas, told his worship staff a couple years ago that he wanted to go to the next level by instituting a holographic type of worship. It had never been done in a church. But by figuring out how to do so, they took worship to a much higher level. The church projected a hologram-like image using six different projectors. It was a few minutes into the message before the congregation figured out what was going on. Ed Young wasn't there. He was a hologram!

Care must be taken when using stretch goals. They can be terribly overwhelming and unattainable if they are too unrealistic. They can sap a staff's motivation. So be careful. Make sure staff people understand they will not be held accountable for stretch goals.

It also helps to set some milestones to measure the results along the way. If the goal is to grow the youth attendance by 100 percent over the next two years, it makes sense to have quarterly milestones. In other words, you don't want to go a year without making some kind of evaluation of the progress. One milestone might be to have the youth worship functioning within three months. Another might be to have the small groups operating within the first six months.

If the leader is receiving quarterly or monthly progress reports, problems are addressed before they become serious. If at the end of the first quarter the youth worship isn't operating, adjustments need to be made as to how the youth director is implementing the goal. If after the second quarter no progress has been accomplished, it might be time to consider replacing the person.

Reflection: Pick out some critical ministry in your church that isn't going well and write out a crisp goal with milestones.

Staff Are a Part of Goal Setting

Unless your staff buys into the goal, the odds are it won't happen. So it's important to have conversations with the staff responsible for achieving the goal. They need the opportunity to express their fears and have their questions answered to fine-tune the program or process.

Suppose you and the staff person can't reach an agreement on the goal and milestones. The wise leader will attempt to parse the difference between an honest objection to the goal and simply a fear of attempting something new. The leader has to be willing to listen to the staff person. The leader must avoid unilaterally saying, "This is the way we're going to do it." Staff must be part of the decision, refining the goal to a manageable point. The key here is not to allow the staff person to give in to fear. You want staff people who have little or no fear when it comes to doing something radically different. Fearless staff people are worth their weight in gold.

But what if a staff person insists on doing something that you know won't work? That's where you say the magical word no. It's poor leadership to allow a staff person to pursue a course of action you feel leads nowhere. However, if you're not totally sure it won't work, give the staff person a short leash and say, "Let's try it for x number of days or months, and then reevaluate it to see if we should continue or discontinue the program or action." As the leader, you should have some idea of what you think will work before sitting down to discuss how, where, and when to do something. Failure to do this step usually doesn't end well.

Reflection: When you present a goal with your staff, how do you do it? Do you have a clearly defined set of expectations, goals, and milestones?

Follow Through Is Essential

Follow through is imperative for staffing. If you don't do this, the goals are seldom met. Whether you delegate or empower a person to do ministry, it doesn't mean you can abdicate following through to see how the person is doing.

For our purposes, let's quickly define delegation and empowerment. Delegation is saying, "Here is what I want done, how I want it done, and when I want it done. Keep me in the loop every step of the way." Empowerment is saying, "We have agreed on the expectations, make it happen. Come and see me if you have a problem."

In order to delegate or empower, leaders have to value getting ministry done through others. Bill Tenny-Brittian and I (BE) write about this extensively in the book *Effective Staffing for Vital Churches,* so we won't go into detail here.[2] But we do need to reiterate that there is one primary reason pastors fail to value getting ministry done through others—they enjoy doing ministry and being needed by their members. Such a value is confining to the growth of both the church and the people. This failure makes the church too dependent on the pastor.

The main challenge of an effective leader is giving the work of actual ministry over to the congregation without abandoning them. Give them too much to do, and they burn out; give them too little to do, and they become dependent and complacent.

Of course, some people require more supervision than others, but everyone needs someone at least checking in on them. For example, it's common to delegate with a new staff person rather than empower them. Although there can be various levels of delegation, the overall issue is the staff person has to keep the supervisor informed every step of the way. If a person is empowered, they only need to check in when progress is monitored, when they have a problem, or when they need advice.

Empowerment is the goal with all staff. But never empower a person until they have proved they will do what they say they will, do it the way they say they will, and do it when they say they will. Trust has to be earned before anyone is empowered to do ministry. Trust is earned by constantly delivering positive results over and over. It has nothing to do with whether or not you like the person. Trust is built on what they do over time.

Still, it is impossible to overstate the importance for a staff member to know there is a seasoned veteran available when needed. Just to know someone is available whom you can go to with your problem is of vital importance to staff people. The one who is supervising must lead in a way that staff people know the supervisor is there for them when they need help.

Reflection: Think back over the past. How many times did you not follow up on your expectations and milestones? What happened? What could you have done differently?

Giving Feedback and Coaching

Part of giving clear expectations is providing people with feedback and coaching. The problem is many pastors give the feedback but don't spend the time coaching and encouraging the person. So when you see a staff person failing, you need to step in and have a conversation. Say something like this: "Tell me where I failed you because you're not making the grade, and I'm the one who hired you and has been your coach. So tell me where I could have helped you succeed because right now you are failing, and I can't keep someone on the staff that continues to fail. We are at a crossroad; either we figure out how you can succeed, or I have to let you go."

A good supervisor always hopes for an outcome other than firing a staff person. Too much time, energy, and money have been involved. On the other hand, it is never the goal of a good supervisor to have a staff person who is so needy they become a mission.

Put this on your refrigerator and never stray from it: "Staff should be on a mission and never be a mission." If you have someone who constantly underperforms and you have given that person all the help you can, let that person go as soon as possible. There comes a time when you have to say, "Enough is enough."

Assuming you have provided that person with the necessary resources and coaching, six months is all the time you need to give that person for figuring out how to move their ministry forward. If adequate progress has not been realized by then, it's time to let him or her go.

Here's where supervision in a church differs from supervision in a business. In a business, a supervisor can be ruthless. In a church, a supervisor must always handle accountability and dismissal as gracefully as possible. We speak of it as being graciously ruthless. That is not to say the time never comes when you have to fire someone, but do so with this mentality: "the quicker, the better." Yet, if you are going to err, do so on the side of going the second mile to be an encourager to that failing staff person. Everyone deserves a second chance. No one deserves a third.

That begs a question. Why is it so important to let someone go as soon as you decide it needs to happen? It is because once a staff person becomes aware that you know they can't do the job and you allow them to stay, they have the opportunity to negatively work their networks. Then when you finally let them go, these networks are more upset than they would have been if you had quickly dismissed the person. Conversely, with effective people, relationships grow continually deeper the longer they are on staff as well, with more being accomplished through those relationships.

What do you see when you look at a staff person? Do you see who they are or what they might become? Obviously, it is best for you to see the potential. Isn't this what Jesus did? He took a rag-tag group of misfits and molded them into the people who would transform the world. A good leader should be able to do the same.

Potential is something someone will do in the future with the right kind of coaching. If you're the lead pastor, think of yourself as a coach of a team that could win the Super Bowl of ministry with the right kind of coaching. Roll up your sleeves and become the best coach you can be. If you don't see this as one of your primary roles, then get out of the way. Let someone else lead.

Be a spiritual midwife. Effective leaders understand they can achieve far more through others than they ever could on their own. Never forget, your staff is your church's best asset. Help them grow, and the chances of growing your church and the kingdom improve exponentially. When they are ready and have proved themselves, give them room to spread their wings and fly—even if they outgrow you. You'll be glad you did.

Reflection: How good are you at giving feedback? How could you improve? Do you have staff that need help and/or staff that need room to fly?

Holding Staff Accountable

Goals without accountability are a waste of time because staff won't have a clue as to how they are doing in the eyes of their supervisor. Allowing staff to be in the dark concerning how you feel about their effectiveness is not leadership. Whether you're unhappy or happy with their performance, they should know it.

When leaders fail to hold staff accountable, whether they are succeeding or failing to achieve the goal, it sends a signal to the rest of the staff. If a failing staff person is allowed to continue just as they are, it says to the rest of the staff that the goals were never expected to materialize in the first place. If a failing staff person is called into question, sent away for training, or fired, it says to the staff that setting and attaining goals are important. Or if the person is succeeding and receives recognition, it sends a positive signal to the rest of the staff. If effective staff people are not given recognition or, worse yet, the lead pastor takes responsibility for their achievements, it sends a signal to the staff that they are taken for granted and the lead pastor isn't to be trusted.

We need to emphasize one more point. If a supervisor allows a failing staff person to stay without getting more training or being replaced, it says to the effective staff who are accomplishing their goals that the supervisor isn't a leader because he or she didn't take action when needed. When that happens, effective staff members begin to bail out and look for another place to serve. Effective staff members crave an effective leader. When they decide they don't have one, they look for a new place to serve. On the other hand, if they are ineffective staff, they dig in and try to stay forever because they know they have an easy ride.

Reflection: Here are some questions for reflection:
Do I have it in me to hold people accountable?
Can I fire someone and sleep at night even if it is his or her only income?
Do I avoid uncomfortable conversations with failing staff?

31

Do I find it difficult to spend time with staff members who need some help or encouragement? If I have a staff person who is failing, what could I do to help that person succeed?

Plainly put, the pastor must always ask: *Am I the person for this church at this size or should I move on?*

So what does accountability look like? Ultimately, this is our relationship of obedience to God. What that practically looks like in a church is an accountability structure such as this:

- A lead pastor is accountable to a board.
- A staff member is accountable to a lead pastor or an executive pastor.
- A layperson is usually accountable to the lead pastor, a staff member, or another layperson of that person's choice or ministry affiliation.

For accountability to be effective, two things must always be present: (1) There is a clearly defined path of accountability—everyone knows who his or her supervisor is, and (2) There is a clearly defined set of expectations agreed upon by both parties.

Staff accountability is always somewhat hierarchical, although any good accountability system should have some form of 360-degree evaluation process. Even in a team setting, where give and take is encouraged, the "buck has to stop" somewhere. When people do not do what they say they will do or when they break a clearly defined expectation or biblical principle, they need to be held accountable. The only reason churches have gotten into the behavioral mess most of them are in today is because no one was held responsible for inappropriate behavior.

Mutual trust is essential for accountability to be a healthy tool for personal growth rather than a sledgehammer held over someone's head. Remember, scripture abounds with accountability stories from Ananias and Sapphira to Paul's dismissal of Mark. The more wishy-washy accountability is, the less likely that church is to grow.

We put a high premium on what we call "permission-giving" in churches, meaning that leaders should be empowered to act as long as they abide by the mission, vision, and values (and budget) of the congregation. People want to know how accountability squares with permission-giving. But there's really no problem because permission-giving is not permissiveness. Permission-giving can only happen within the clearly defined boundaries of objectives. It can't violate the agreed-upon goals. So even in a permission-giving environment, accountability is essential for effective and faithful ministry to occur.

Tom Bandy, a former partner in our firm, has one of the best examples of how accountability works today as opposed to how it worked in the past:

> Speaking metaphorically, this is the difference between training dogs and raising rabbits. In the old world, we trained dogs (task groups and committees) to fetch, roll over, and do programs. The leash on the dog was the long prescriptive job description that told the task group what they had to do and how they h~ to do it. If the dog didn't do what you wanted, you jerke~' chain, and appealed to the bylaws. If the task group ' obediently, you gave the dog a pat on the head. Th~ any dog owner wants is a creative dog!

In the new world, we raise rabbits (teams and cell groups). You can't put a leash on a rabbit, but you have to build a fence. These are the boundaries within which the rabbits are free to roam, but beyond which they cannot run. These are the core values, beliefs, vision, and mission of the organization. In addition, you fence off any vegetable patch or other vulnerable area in order to protect safety and confidentiality, guide the rabbits in continuing education, or keep rabbits from getting in each other's way. These are the executive limitations. The very first thing we want is for the rabbits to be as creative and innovative as possible![3]

Clear boundaries have to be in place for accountability to be successful. However, the most effective boundaries are permeable. There must be considerable freedom to act within the given boundaries. Set them, make sure everyone knows them, and let staff people run free as long as they stay within the boundaries. They have to be clear enough to know when they have been crossed and broad enough to allow a person to be creative.

One of the best books on setting such boundaries is *The Boundaryless Organization*.[4] It offers practical hints for how to evaluate the boundaries that are harmful to the health of an organization and to reform the way the church organizes and functions. Step-by-step practical help is offered to those church leaders wanting to break old, unhealthy patterns and create new, healthy patterns of behavior.

Let's go back to the example used earlier. *By January 2015, grow the youth attendance by 100 percent using youth worship on Sunday and small groups that create new servant leaders.* A permeable boundary is "grow the youth program by 100 percent over the next three years through worship and small groups." Notice nothing is said about how worship and small groups are to be done. There is a clear boundary set with lots of room to roam as long as the focus is on worship and small groups that grow the youth program and create new leaders.

Reflection: What are the boundaries in which your staff has a lot of freedom to act?

Understanding Execution

You've read a lot now about execution, so let's do an exercise to see how well you understand the concept.

Joe is responsible for the youth ministry. He and the pastor had a long conversation before setting any goals. The pastor shared a clear expectation—double the number of participating youth within two years. The "hows" were through youth worship and small groups that grow the church and create new leaders. Milestones were put in place—10 percent the first three months, 30 percent the next six months, 40 percent the next six months, and 20 percent the last three months. He was supposed to report the progress to the pastor at each milestone. After a lengthy conversation, the youth pastor bought into all of the above. At the end of twenty-four months, the youth group grew by 10 percent and the youth director was still on the staff.

Refection: What went wrong? See if you can figure it out before reading further.

The pastor must take the blame for allowing the youth program to linger for two years. The pastor had the reports and knew

35

the youth director was going to miss the first milestone, so there should have been a conversation when the first milestone was not reached about what was going wrong and what could be done to help. After the first quarter, there were two choices—get the youth director some help or let him go. Allowing the person to remain on the staff simply made everyone's job harder, and the pastor ran the risk of losing face with other staff members for not taking action.

If things aren't going well at your church, it's best to first look in the mirror to find the solution. What could you be doing wrong or not doing? Perhaps you:

- Work in your own tiny silo.
- Haven't set clear expectations and goals.
- Haven't shared your vision to the point that it sticks.
- Haven't selected the right people for the right job.
- Allowed unproductive people to stay on the staff too long.
- Haven't held staff accountable.
- Didn't offer feedback.
- Have failed to listen to feedback.
- Have excessively dabbled in their day-to-day ministry.
- Have delegated or empowered when you shouldn't have.
- Abdicated availability.

It has to be one or more of the above. The responsibility is always on the lead pastor or executive pastor.

Priesthood of the Individual

In order to execute a vision, anyone responsible for a section of ministry must learn how to hand off some aspects to others.

Even though you may know you can do it better than anyone else, you can only do so much. Learning how to multiply yourself is one of the most important lessons a leader can learn in life.

Most pastors have trouble making this shift from depending on self to depending on others to get ministry done. The primary reason is the pastor's desire to feel needed. When a leader hoards the responsibility for a ministry, they are robbing others of the joy to be found from fulfilling God's mission in the world.

So what attitude must a leader have to effectively hand off ministry?

- Leaders have to believe that every person feels better about himself or herself when they contribute to the overall success of the organization. This feeling is especially true for Christians. We are made to be involved with God in the great mission of the redemption of creation. No one grows or finds true fulfillment sitting in a pew being hand-fed. Playing the game is ultimately more fulfilling than sitting in the stands watching.

- Leaders have to believe in the priesthood of the individual. God has something for every Christian to do with his or her life. Finding that one thing is the most fulfilling event in a Christian's life.

- Leaders have to revel in the success of others and the small part they played in it.

- Leaders must match each person to a ministry that feeds them as well as the people they are serving. Too many pastors treat volunteers as if they were pawns in a game to help pastors grow the church or take a load off. Instead, leaders must think of those they are responsible for as servants in search of a God-given mission.

It is vital that pastors realize they are responsible for the success or failure of the staff. Execution begins and ends with the leader.

Reflection: Do you honor the priesthood of the individual? If not, what do you need to do or change to make this happen?

The Role of the Leader in Execution

I n a constantly changing world, the role of a leader is also constantly changing. Leaders have to learn new ways of thinking and acting, develop new skills, embrace new paradigms, integrate left and right brain thinking, become skilled politicians, see old things in new ways, and be a team player. If you're serious about growing a church, that very lengthy list should get your attention. So let's try to simplify that role.

Behind all of the execution items in the previous chapter, two actions regarding the vision of the leader take precedent over all other traits: (1) The pastor maintains focus on the vision, and (2) The pastor keeps the staff similarly focused. Let's explore what that looks like.

Be Focused on the Vision

The essential role of the leader is to stay focused on the vision. Churches have a way of taking everyone's eyes off the prize, especially the pastor's. There are so many things to do and so many people who want some of the pastor's time that being able to keep a proper focus is a challenge. Ineffective pastors give into the pressure of the crowd. If the leader allows this to happen to him or her, the same will happen with the staff. So one of the key roles of the leader is to keep everyone focused on the vision and the goal. Like a dog with a bone, the leader relentlessly focuses on the overall priorities that keep everyone moving forward to achieve their goals.

The ability to stay focused when everyone around you is clamoring for their fair share of your time is one of the greatest challenges we've seen in lead pastors, especially in the small to midsized church. The smaller the church, the harder it is to stay focused on the vision.

The only way the pastor can remain focused on the vision and avoid the distracting voices of the crowd, without ignoring them, is to always lead from the sideline with one foot in the game and one foot out of it. What does that look like?

Perhaps Magic Johnson's greatest contribution to the game of basketball came from his ability to play hard while keeping in mind the whole strategy of the game, as if he were in the stands watching. He not only knew what he was supposed to do but also what everyone else was supposed to do. He had a ten thousand foot view of the court. That is what the effective leader has to be able to do.

Few people in a church, other than the pastor and perhaps a few key staff, understand the total ramifications of the big vision. A lead pastor has to be so consumed by the vision that he or she can see the vision from a ten-thousand-foot perspective without losing sight of the players. A lead pastor brings that vision onto the playing field where each player knows his or her role in implementing the vision.

To keep their focus on the vision, leaders will both participate and observe. By seeing the ministry from ten thousand feet, leaders avoid getting caught up in the multitude of voices and the day-to-day issues. They are aware of those voices, and sometimes they listen to those voices, but they never allow those voices to distract them from the vision.

Sounds easy? It's not. The threat here is that many pastors have a high mercy gift. The higher the mercy gift pastors have, the easier it is for them to lose focus and be diverted by one person instead of being consumed by the vision. Or we could put it this way—too many pastors are consumed more by their mercy gift than they are by the vision. The gift of mercy is wonderful, but mercy in the leadership role can be deadly.

Studies show that few people can stay focused on more than four priorities at a time. Most people can focus on only one or two priorities at a time. See the problem? The priorities in a church are legion if you allow everyone to speak into your life. You have to not only choose your priorities but also to whom you listen.[1]

I (BE) consulted with a church over two decades ago that had been in decline for thirty years. Once a very large church, it had decreased to around three hundred in worship. After being there for three days, I left them with seven recommendations. I prefaced the seven recommendations with this warning: "Not accomplishing the first recommendation means failure for the church no matter how well you do with the remaining six."

A year later, I received a letter (that was before e-mail). The letter said, "We've accomplished six out of the seven goals, and we are still declining. We haven't tackled the first recommendation because we're afraid of splitting the church (the first recommendation was starting a new indigenous worship service). What advice do you have?"

I wrote back and filled the entire letter with one word over and over—"Focus." Then I finished the letter with something like this: "Accomplish the first recommendation! Failure to do so will mean you will fail as pastor of the church." The pastor finally took my advice, and when he left some twenty years later, the worship attendance was above eleven hundred. All because of one tiny word that is so hard for most pastors—FOCUS!

What does it mean to have focus? Focus is the ability to shut out every other option, voice, choice, or direction. It is the ability to be so sure about what you are doing and where you are going that nothing distracts you. Focus for a leader is like putting blinders on a horse. The blinders keep the horse focused on one thing, looking forward—not seeing all the hazards or competition that surrounds it. To be a leader in today's noisy world, you have to have this kind of focus.

Reflection: So what are the four priorities upon which you have to focus? Take a moment to think about them, and write them down. Then choose one of them as your real priority for the moment. What is your strategy for making it happen?

Keep the Staff Focused

A follow-up priority of the lead pastor is to keep the staff focused on the execution of the vision. Staff people are like anyone else. They can get distracted, especially if they have needy people in their area of responsibility. Holding people accountable to executing the vision is essential. If you don't measure it, it likely won't get done.

Reflection: How are you doing with keeping your focus on the vision? Does the vision dictate how you spend your time or does something else? Does your staff stay focused on the vision?

EQ Trumps IQ

Keeping focused on a few priorities when everyone around you has a different opinion requires an enormous amount of confidence that comes only from emotional stability on the part of the leader. So let's unpack what that means.

Some pastors are smarter than most, and yet they can't figure out how to help their churches grow. Some pastors are not as smart as others, and their churches are growing. What's the difference?

Our experience, and that of many others, tells us that the difference doesn't have as much to do with IQ (Intelligence Quotient) as it does with EQ (Emotional Quotient). For example, Einstein was a genius, but he wasn't a leader. Stop for a moment, and consider that statement.

Although a high IQ certainly doesn't hurt, it isn't the main ingredient in growing a church or being a leader. How much a person knows is great if you're playing a game of trivia or trying to solve a mathematical problem, but it takes a backseat to EQ when it comes to leadership and execution. What matters is how badly you want something to happen, and how much you believe in your vision. EQ is something you have to either learn or have thrust upon you like a religious experience. In the case of a pastor, it can be a recently attended seminar, a book, or an all-encompassing call that focuses the pastor on the Great Commission.

EQ is what moves others to action. So it's often not what you say but how you say it. Consider the following famous words that rocked nations:

- Martin Luther: *"Here I stand. I can do no other."*
- Martin Luther King Jr: *"I have a dream."*
- Ronald Reagan: *"Mr. Gorbachev, tear down this wall."*
- Franklin D. Roosevelt: *"We have nothing to fear, but fear itself."*

In the face of seemingly impossible odds, these men had the courage of their conviction and stood by their vision to the point that it moved mountains. That's the power of the motivation that comes from EQ.

EQ has two components: what it does to you and what it does to others. When it is intense, it gives you the courage to stand by your conviction and prompts others to join in the journey. EQ also allows a leader to receive criticism without taking it personally or, worse, taking it home.

Of course, like most things, a powerful EQ can be used for both good and ill. Hitler is a case in point. He had tremendous EQ, and the masses flocked to him. Unfortunately, many pastors use such examples as excuses for not using the power of EQ to encourage church members to do what the scriptures say needs to be done. But that's their problem. Effective leaders know that the use of power is a neutral action. It can be good or bad, but failure to exercise one's God-given ability is a serious mistake for any leader. A good leader has to use power when controllers or bullies try to hijack the vision and turn the church inward on itself, becoming more of a club than a church. More on the use of power later.

Of course, IQ is important, and we don't mean to belittle it. But IQ doesn't move mountains, and we've got mountains to move these days. The results of several studies done in some major corporations have shown that EQ is 80 to 90 percent of what separates the average leader from the exceptional leader.

Reflect on these questions: How much do you believe in your vision? How much does your staff believe in the vision? To what lengths are you willing to go to make it happen, and how well have the leaders bought into the vision? Does the staff understand the expectations and goals? How much does the staff believe in the goals?

Instead of asking the above questions, most pastors and boards ask questions like this: Will it work? Is it feasible? Can we do it? Can we afford it? The problem is, in such an uncertain time as ours, no one knows the answers to these questions. So instead of thinking through a problem, leaders have to feel their way along. Once having all the possible data, leaders let intuition and faith take over to guide their decision. In times like these, you won't know what will work until you take action. As Nike says, "Just do it." Take that first step. See what happens. You either fail and learn a lesson about what doesn't work (which gives you a leg up on what might work) or you succeed and move ahead as if you knew what you were doing all the time. Either way, you are on the road to being more effective.

Case in point: do you think Jeff Bezos knew his Amazon venture would work? No way, because no one else had done it. But did he believe it would work? So much so that he put up all the money he had. What allowed him to take such a bold action? His intuition told him he had to do it, and he totally believed it would work.

When I (BE) restarted the church I stayed at for twenty-four years, I went without a salary for a year. Why? Not because I knew the church would grow, but because I believed our strategy would work. I've seen many church planters do the same. They use their own money to start the church. They spend all of their savings; not because they know it's a shoo-in, but because they passionately believe in what they are doing. In fact, they believe it is what God put them on this planet to accomplish.

So how do you know if your EQ is high enough? That's a tough question to answer, but let's try.

How self-aware are you? By that we mean three things: (1) How in tune are you with your feelings and how they impact your performance? (2) Do you know your limitations, being open to candidly talking about them? (3) Do you lean into your strengths more than trying to improve your weaknesses? This is why we constantly remind pastors to trust their gut and never abandon their call. It is also why the more focused a call is for a pastor, the more likely he or she is to be an exceptional leader.

How in control are you of your daily life? Are you calm under pressure and never seem to be rattled? Are you able to adapt when necessary to reach a goal? When confronted with new options or information, are you able to suspend judgment long enough to give an intelligent response? Are you pragmatic in your goals with higher standards for yourself than for others? Are you confident enough to seek ways to improve your performance?

How socially aware are you? Do you have enough empathy with people that you tune into what they are feeling? Are you politically astute enough to be able to read key power relationships? Are you constantly monitoring the well-being of those for whom you are responsible?

How do you manage relationships? Do your actions inspire others to act? Are you adept at cultivating other people's abilities? When faced with opposition, can you still inspire courage and help others stand their ground? Are you able to manage conflict by bringing out the best in others? Are you collegial in your relationships, fostering teamwork and collaboration?

Of course, very few people have all of these gifts, but the more of them a person has, the higher their EQ will be.

Reflection: As you look over the list, can you see how EQ prepares a person to lead far more effectively than IQ? Which one on the list is your greatest strength?

Learning to Develop Intuition

It should be clear by now that traditional thinking and acting aren't going to give us the results we seek. We have to first know the facts. Then once we've gathered the data, we take action based on our best guess—we're back to the foundational leadership quality of intuition.

Just like skills, intuition can be developed. And just like with skills, some people will develop intuition better than others. In both cases, if a person doesn't work on them, they don't improve. Our experience with pastors is that they are some of the least intuitive people. However, it may not be fully their fault.

The primary reason pastors have trouble with developing intuition is the way we have been taught to learn or, should we say, taught not to learn. Most ministerial education today is the teacher talks and the students diligently listen while taking copious notes.

There is a name for this kind of learning—it's called "passive learning." Passive learning doesn't teach us how to analyze. We learn the facts, but not what they mean to our everyday life. That's why, in this book, you have been asked several times to stop reading and reflect. People learn more about what works by doing rather than by hearing or reading.

Case in point: why do you think Mark Zuckerberg and Bill Gates dropped out of Harvard to follow their vision? They intuitively believed that their dreams were more important than a Harvard education.

Sixteen years ago, I (SM) had this nagging gut feeling that I was supposed to pursue a program at the Wagner Leadership Institute in Colorado Springs, a Spirit-driven seminary that would be outside what had been my comfort zone. C. Peter Wagner started this institution in his senior years because he wanted to develop an educational program that used a style other than the one he had utilized previously at Fuller Seminary.

I'll be honest. I hated to speak spontaneous prayers. That's not good when you are a pastor. I felt my unscripted prayers sounded stilted. I had no idea why God seemed to want me to go to this institution. But I went nonetheless.

The learning practice was far different than that of my past. What I came away with was a powerful new sense of prayer that now drives all of my life. These people didn't teach me to pray. They put me in an experience where I was mentored to become the person of prayer God wanted. So, especially at a time when the questions are many and the answers seem few, we encourage you to step out of your comfort zone for the sake of Jesus. This leads us to the issue of how well you are applying the lessons in this book.

Our bet is most of you didn't stop reading and reflect on the questions. So you will get to the end of the book and have your head full of information, but you still may not be better prepared to turn a vision into reality. Have you done the exercises so far? If not, we encourage you to go back and do them now.

Reflection: Analyze your preaching. Do you preach for a specific response from the congregation? If not, you are encouraging passive listening, which seldom leads to action.

Pastors need to take part in "active learning," which prepares them to read the signs of the times and know how to act intuitively. Active learning is an approach to instruction in which students engage the material they study through reading, writing, talking, listening, reflecting, and doing. Active learning has been described as a process whereby students engage in a higher order of thinking tasks such as analysis, synthesis, and evaluation.[2] Active learning stands in contrast to "standard" models of instruction in which teachers do most of the talking and students passively receive. A passive approach to books or lectures is much less effective than an active one in which you ask and answer questions, challenge the author, and relate the material to your own experience.

Math is one of the best examples of active learning. Students are required to solve a problem. They have been instructed in how to solve it, but they must demonstrate they understand the concepts behind the solution. Even today, pastors are rarely asked to solve potential ministry issues at traditional seminaries. If you do the reflections throughout this book, you have a great opportunity for personal growth. You might improve your intuition.

Learning Pyramid

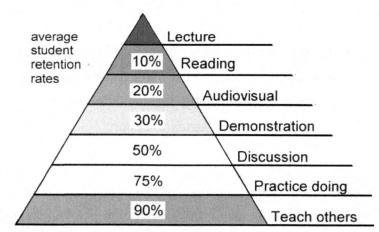

Source: NTL Institute for Applied Behavioral Science

From the graphic above, you will see how instruction improves with actual participation on the part of the student.

You will hear us say: "You don't think your way into a new way of thinking; you act your way into a new way of thinking." If we don't know for sure what will work in the new world, all we can do is take a leap of faith. Maybe that's why Jesus sent the disciples out two by two to gain hands-on experience in the most important thing they would do when he left—make disciples.

Where Power Resides

By this time you may be thinking, "But aren't you giving too much power to the pastor?" Our unequivocal answer is no.

We've met pastors who want their church to grow but don't want to be the leader, because they don't want to exercise any power or authority. The problem is this never works. Growth takes a leader who is so convinced of the outcome that he or she influences others to jump on board and use their gifts to help make the vision happen.

What many don't understand is that in a church someone always exercises power, either for good or bad. In the absence of a leader who exercises good power, controllers or bullies usually step into the vacuum and exercise bad power. That always causes a church to stall or decline.

Please don't suggest that pastors should refrain from using power because of instances when such leaders have abused their position. Laypeople have misused power far more times and much more detrimentally than pastors. So use the power God has given you, always remembering that what has been given can be taken away if it is abused.

Power Versus Authority

At this point, it's important to define how we understand power. The kind of power most pastors are afraid of is having the ability to make others conform to something against their will. In this understanding, power comes from some form of dominance based on coercion. That's not the way we're using the term *power*.

To us, power is more like authority. Authority is based on relationships that are voluntary and conscious. Authority emerges when leaders consistently demonstrate they have the best interest of others in mind so that people are willing to join them on the journey. The wrong use of power constrains a person's will, while the right use of power encourages and transforms their will. Knowing the difference is part of what makes a leader effective. This is a person who isn't afraid to use the power that comes from being given authority.

The world before the fourth transition mentality located power in a *role* rather than a *person*. The pastor had respect and therefore some amount of authority just by being the pastor. After the fourth transition, people are not willing to give power to a role. Now authority has to be earned by a person. People have to trust leaders enough to ascribe power to them.

Before the fourth transition, authority was more of a straight line than it is today. Children obeyed their parents. Employees did what their employer told them to do, and so on. Power was invested in rules. But today, the kind of authority that leads to power is more relational than linear. It is earned by what the leader does over time as well as how the leader invests in the potential of others.

Here is the tricky part. Instead of authority coming from what a person takes, now it comes from what a person gives. The leader who delegates and empowers others to achieve, even beyond the leader, is the one who gains respect and authority.

The effective pastor knows that the best way to succeed is to help others succeed. The effective pastor knows that the path to authority does not come by way of the degree on the wall but by how consistently he or she leads—the more effective the leader, the more authority is granted.

One of the best books over the past decade on authority and how it develops is *Reworking Authority* by Larry Hirschhorn. It is helpful in explaining to parents, grandparents, CEOs, and pastors why they don't receive the respect they often feel they deserve. In his book the author argues that in times of great change, like we are experiencing today, it is necessary to create a new kind of authority—one in which superiors acknowledge their dependence on subordinates, subordinates can challenge their superiors, and both are able to show vulnerability.[3]

How then, you ask, does a leader gain respect, authority, or power? The answer is simple—by consistently doing the things that lead the organization to greater effectiveness, by empowering people to reach the zenith of their potential. Leaders gain a following by consistently pointing out the direction to a better future and by developing leaders that thrive.

There is a book on power, *Playing God: Redeeming the Gift of Power*, which offers some further insight on authority. Here is a quote for your consideration.

> Why is power a gift? Because power is for flourishing. When power is used well, people and the whole cosmos come more alive to what they were meant to be. And flourishing is the test of power.[4]

When used to further the kingdom, whether you call it power or authority, it is a gift from God that we dare not let go unused.

To share the Gospel in a way that helps people thrive is the most powerful act a person can make. We hope you will begin thinking about power as a gift from God and not be afraid to use it wisely.

Reflection: How do you feel about the use of power/authority? Are you reluctant to use it? Are you afraid of abusing it?

Leading without Ruling

If we understand the issues involved with power, then we know that there is an unspoken covenant involved. People give authority to a leader. It is retained so long as the leader continues leading in the way that earned him or her that privilege.

In the book *Accountability*, the authors write, "The key is to find a way to lead people without ruling them."[5] For us, the key to accomplishing this is two-fold: (1) To have a vision so compelling that people are enthralled by it, and (2) free people to work in self-organized, self-governed, self-destructing teams. I (BE) talked about how this happens in my book *Sacred Cows Make Gourmet Burgers*.[6]

Don't be afraid to exercise power, but be careful not to abuse it. The temptation to do so grows with tenure. The longer you are pastor of a church, the more tempted you can be to abuse your authority. You've earned credibility. This is where the temptation emerges. Never try to overuse your status and privilege as the leader. Remember what is given can be taken away. God doesn't honor the abuse of power.

Reflection: Remember the last time you had to exercise your authority. How did it make you feel, and what did you learn about yourself?

Leaders Must Lead

To be successful as a leader you have to lead. We have learned that if a problem exists, it *always* resides at the feet of the leader. For example: if the choir has a problem, it is the choir director's fault. If the children's area is not going well, it is the children's director's fault. Change the leader, and the ministry has a chance to improve.

I (BE) had this truth driven home to me my first few years of my restart effort. I started a preschool the second year, and two years later there were only four children. The new church was drowning in red ink. I replaced the director, and by the third year eighty-five children were enrolled. Remember—the problem is always the leader.

There are two questions you have to ask yourself. They are: "Who am I?" and "What did God put me here to do?" You have to be able to answer these two questions in order to develop the type of passion it takes to lead. If you know who you are, you have some hint of your limitations or weaknesses. If you know what God put you here to do, you have a holy passion or desire to make it happen.

I (SM) mentioned before that I asked these questions of myself twenty years ago. It was a transforming moment when a vision pointed me in the direction of a new reality. Make no mistake;

this is the ministry of Jesus who requires you to pick up a cross to execute your vision. It's bumpy. There will be conflict. People will leave your church. You must remain focused and grounded in spiritual discipline with your sight on the destination.

God shows in the Bible that he honors persistence. That is a part of leading without distraction. Twenty years ago, Bill Easum was an icon to me. I read his words more than those of anyone else. Now I am a coauthor on a book with him and a partner in the church consulting firm he started. I sure didn't see that coming, and that is the delight of your vision coming to God's desired fruition.

The Seduction of Leadership

Now we need to explain the difference between a manager and a leader, showing how an overemphasis on management has seduced pastors and churches away from the primary vision of making disciples.

Management is the process of keeping the machinery of an organization running smoothly. It includes items such as budgeting, planning, organizing, and problem-solving. Leadership, in contrast, is the process of defining the future, setting the direction, aligning people with the vision, finding the right people, putting them in the right place, and inspiring them to execute goals.

Let's look at management and leadership in the light of the Key to Everything.

With the rise of large institutions in the twentieth century, the greatest need was for managers who could hold it all together. For every entrepreneur, the culture needed hundreds of managers. So management programs were created to turn out better managers. As a result, very little emphasis was given to leadership. This lack of emphasis was especially true in seminaries.

Shift gears to today. Because of the speed and discontinuity of change, now the church's pressing need is for people who can lead into the emerging new world. But it is universally agreed upon by church officials that the number of pastors who can lead in this manner is significantly lacking.

Reflection: Which trait is your strongest, management or leadership? Do you possess both of them? How does this impact your ability to move your congregation into the future?

Two Primary Examples

A helpful way to explain what has happened in most churches is to use the example of the average new church start. In the beginning, the pastor and the church are outwardly focused. The emphasis is on reaching out to and bringing in new people. Because there is no infrastructure and many of the people are new to Christianity, the pastor has to assume the role of leader. If the pastor is successful, the church grows.

It's at this point that the seduction occurs. The church members want the pastor to spend more time taking care of them and developing programs. Increasingly, the pastor's attention turns from being outwardly focused to spending more and more time managing the internal concerns of the church—taking care of the members. Guess what? The church stops growing, and decline begins.

The sad truth is that too many pastors have poor management skills. They haven't had any training, and their passion is more for people than organization. As a result, they rarely succeed at much

57

more than being a pastoral caregiver. Over time, even the word *leader* causes raised eyebrows and suspicion.

An example of this seduction occurred in the United Methodist Church. Methodism in the United States was one of the most successful missionary movements in history. Over a few decades, the Methodist Church reached from the East to West Coasts. The primary vehicle of this movement was the itinerant circuit rider. They would ride in and preach then ride out to the next church. They didn't take care of the flock; the flock took care of itself. None of these circuit riders had any training. They just had a passion to spread the Gospel.

But in the mid-to-late 1950s, it was decided that clergy needed to be formally educated and seminary training began. As people graduated, they were given a church and taught how to care for a congregation. Over time they were given a bigger church. The more the pastors played the party line and politics, the higher they moved in the system until some became bishops.

Most of these bishops were good at managing an organized church. Very few of them were part of a growing church; they just managed what they had been given. Now, as bishops, they honor and understand management. But pastors who are strong leaders often threaten bishops and may be viewed as mavericks. See the depth of the problem—leadership is not only suspect, but to some, it's the enemy.

Reflection: Have you been seduced into simply managing the institution? If so, what are you going to do about it?

Addressing the Leadership Vacuum

How do we confront this leadership vacuum? First, we must agree that leadership is more caught than taught. We're convinced the desire for leadership comes from a deep sense of call—a call so clear and overpowering that it erases all forms of fear. It's like Jesus told the disciples in Luke 12:12: "The Holy Spirit will tell you at that very moment what you must say." In other words, a person is so pumped that they have no choice except to lead.

But there's more to it than just the call, even if it all begins there. Let's take a look at what leadership entails in a changing world like ours.

Leading During Transitions

It is our sense that leaders are managers, but not all managers are leaders. If you can't manage, then get out of the way. This isn't the way most people think of pastors.

The myth is that pastors are shepherds who take care of people. In reality, that is far from the New Testament plan for pastors. The New Testament expects pastors to equip people to take care of each other. Effective pastors are good managers as well as leaders, or they have learned they need an executive pastor who functions as a manager, like Jethro did for Moses. The problem is that most churches don't get big enough to afford an executive pastor. So the problem continues, and the church declines.

Leading a church is hard enough without having to manage the outcome during a major transition in history. But that is where pastors find themselves today. It's not that we just have to manage; we have to manage on the fly. We don't have the luxury of taking time out to think about our next move. Instead we must act our way into the future. Please focus on this last sentence. Keep this in your head—you act your way into the future; you don't think your way into the future. Taking action is at the heart of being a leader.

One of the things that has frustrated us over the years about pastors is their inability to act. They know something needs to be done, but they won't do it. Have you ever had that problem?

Say for example a church is out of worship space, and the pastor knows an additional service is in order. But a year, two years, three years pass, and still the additional service isn't started. The pastor has given it a lot of thought. Several meetings have been held to talk about how to do the service, but it never gets done. There are always more people to get on board first.

Or take another example. One of the staff members has been performing poorly for some time. The pastor has talked with the person several times, but there is no improvement. Several years go by, and that same person remains on the staff. The pastor simply can't fire the person.

The reasons for inaction are legion, but one stands out above all the rest. Most pastors don't have a burning *desire* to fulfill God's mission for the church that consumes every waking moment. They enjoy ministry because it makes them feel good, but seeing the Great Commission accomplished is not their highest priority.

When Moses went up into the mountain to seek out God, do you think anything would have distracted him from his search? When Jesus went to the cross, do you think there was anything that would have swayed him? When Paul set out to change the world, do you think anyone could have convinced him otherwise? The answer is simple. No. What about you?

When you set out to get something completed that you know should be done, can you put aside everything else? Effective leaders will not allow anything to distract them from their quest to accomplish what they know is the right thing to do.

Desire for kingdom growth is the goal for effective church leadership—desire to please God, desire to accomplish what God put you here to do, and desire to see the kingdom come on earth. Desire is the most potent weapon we have against an inability to act.

Now here are some questions for you to consider. What do you dream about at night? What do you think about when you wake up? What keeps you awake at night? What occupies most of your day? What is the one thing you want to happen more than anything else? The totality of those questions is what you desire. And if they are all different, then more than likely an overwhelming kingdom desire isn't present in your life, and you're not effectively leading your church.

There was a pastor who knew that a parking lot was standing in the way of his church growing. He *really* wanted that parking lot. He knew it was one of his main goals. The problem is the everyday responsibilities got in the way. He was easily distracted. He couldn't stay focused to the point that his desire to see it happen overshadowed everything else. He wanted it, needed it, but he didn't desire it.

You see, church leadership boils down to one thing—how badly do you want your church to grow? Or how convinced are you that the church is the sign of God's kingdom on earth?

What is it you desire the most in life—a great marriage, a healthy life, a good car, or doing God's will? Where does God's will stack up in your life? More specifically, when you know something

61

needs to be done to advance the kingdom, do you desire it enough to prevent anything getting in the way of its fulfillment?

Reflection: Are you able to act without thinking about it for a long time?

Two Axioms for Acting

1) Distractions dilute passion. Don't kid yourself. Distractions can derail even the most focused person, especially in a church setting where so many members expect the pastor to provide spiritual care for them.

2) Focus fuels passion. The more a person focuses on something, the more that person is passionate about seeing it fulfilled, and the quicker that person acts. When passion for something consumes a person's waking moments, the odds are that something is going to happen.

So how does one become consumed with passion for a particular action?

Here are some principles that lead to action:

- You get what you look for.
- The more you look, the more you see.
- The more you see, the more options you see.
- The more options you see, the more excited you get.
- The more excited you get, the more passionate you become.
- The more passionate you become, the more likely you are to act.

But it all breaks down if you don't first look beyond your nose.

Let's use the new worship service example again. When the idea of an additional service surfaces, most pastors will not, notice we did not say cannot, set aside enough time to focus on the idea. After all, there is so much to do; so many meetings; so many people needing care. The pastor knows what needs to be done but isn't willing to focus on it to the point that it becomes a reality.

But now take on the role of the pastor who knows that an additional service is essential to the future of the church. The more you think and pray about it, the more you work toward the completion of the project, even at the expense of other important duties. At first, there isn't a clue how, when, or where this service will take place. All you know is that it has to happen. The more you focus on the service, the more options you see. The service could be in the worship center or the fellowship hall, or in a strip mall down the street. It could be by remote or simultaneously by speaking at one service early and the other service late. With so many options staring you in the face, you now get excited. This service really is a possibility. We can do this! You get so excited that you bypass the committees, gather the musicians, print the flyers, and start the service.

Reflection: When was the last time you bypassed procedure and just did it?

Managing through Transitions

Today's world requires leaders to manage three elements of change if they want to keep themselves sane and their church growing. Let's take a look at them.

1) Leaders Must Manage Themselves. Pastors or executive pastors have to be flexible on the nonessentials and stubborn on the essentials. Let's use worship again as the example. If a person is looking, it is impossible to miss the rise of new styles of music and the use of visuals in our culture, especially among those who are younger. To be an effective manager of worship, pastors must embrace these even if they don't like them and still remain true to their biblical convictions. They have to be comfortable with the idea that the style of worship has nothing whatsoever to do with any biblical position. Any style can convey the Gospel. Unless you can agree with this last statement, your future is in jeopardy.

This means pastors must learn how to put their own opinions and prejudices aside in order to respond to the emerging culture. The good manager wants the culture to grow into their style rather than their style to grow into the culture. The effective pastor is always adapting ahead of the culture while remaining steadfast in basic biblical principles.

Willow Creek Church in Chicago is a good example of allowing the culture to grow into them. They focused on seeker worship long before the media picked up on the secularization of the United States. They intuitively knew that a growing number of people wouldn't respond to traditional forms of worship. So they developed a different style for a new generation of worshipers.

I (BE) remember interviewing Adam Hamilton, pastor of the Church of the Resurrection in Kansas City. The congregation began with a traditional form of worship. When I asked Adam about it, he said, "If I had started this church on the other side of town, it most likely would have been a country western style of worship." [7]

Those who will set the pace of the future will adapt ahead of the culture. They will read the signs of the time, let their intuition take over, and ride the wave into the future.

2) Leaders Must Manage Their Networks. One of the things we are quickly learning about the new world is that two minds are better than one, and four are better than two, and so on. The new world is complicated. It's rare to find the solo leader who functions totally in his or her own vacuum. Most of the great leaders we've seen surround themselves with a host of gifted people who are on the same quest as the leader. So don't be afraid of gifted people. Instead, surround yourself with them. The more gifted your networks, the more likely you and the church are to succeed in its mission.

These networks can be friends, coworkers, or enemies. In our case, we are mostly referring to paid and unpaid staff. They are your church's most valuable resource. If you learn how to network them, you have significantly raised your ability to accomplish things. With the right relationships, you can generate success. But success won't happen overnight. In fact, it may take years. That's why it is important for you to continuously build relationships. Once you have established credibility and trust within your networks, you can reach out to them for help.

To get started, make a list of all the various people, groups, websites, churches, and so on that form your web of networks. Don't forget social media. It's not just social; it's taking networking to the next level.

Next, rate them by the extent of their influence. Some will be wider than others. Some will be more influential monetarily. Some will be limited in both reach and influence; those will obviously receive less of your time.

Direct your attention to the collective experience of the most impactful networks. You will be surprised how much people want to help. However, before you ask for help, make sure that you are first providing value to your networks. Spend time nurturing those relationships and being there for them when they need you.

You will be amazed at what can happen when you leverage your network. Having gathered a group of gifted people, leaders now manage them in ways to bring out the collective best.

3) Leaders Must Manage a Great Team. For our purpose, we will define a team as "a small group of people with complementary skills, who have affinity for one another, who are invited, not elected, by an individual to: achieve a common goal which supersedes individual interests, integrate their skills, and hold each other accountable to the goal."

The most important thing to understand about a great team is that it is an entrepreneurial partnership between the leader and the group. If our world were still predictable and slowly evolving, we would not need such teams. We would utilize a task force, an agency, a staff of professionals, or maybe even a committee. But that's not the way our world is.

If we want to find our way in the cultural jungle of blur, flux, and speed, we need an entrepreneurial A-team. These teams are made up of autonomous individuals who choose to form alliances and networks with others. It is the role of the leader to ensure these teams promote the vision of the church.

Great teams work best in web-like organizations that function around a clearly defined and agreed upon DNA—Mission, Vision, Values, and Beliefs. They do poorly in highly rigid, top-down hierarchical organizations. Therefore, the leader has to be able to lead without ruling. The problem is that pastors often either keep hands-off or micromanage. Either style is deadly in today's world.

Still, at the center of every great team we find a profound leader. A great leader makes a mediocre team great, and a mediocre leader makes a great team mediocre. Teams are only effective when there is the presence and influence of a strong leader. Teams do not replace the need for an entrepreneurial individual at the center of the organization.

In their book *The Paradox Principles*, the Price Waterhouse team reported on their study of several major successful organizations.[8] In this study, they found that every effective team-based ministry had an extremely capable leader at the center of the organization. Our experience is that in the absence of a strong leader, the negative aspects of the organization always take control.

Reflection: Which of the three areas of management give you the most trouble?

Never Look in the Rearview Mirror

We can't lead or manage by looking in the rearview mirror because what once worked probably won't work today. We have to anticipate the future and act accordingly. This is taking a calculated risk. That's where management and intuition cross paths. Statistics are one thing. Interpreting statistics in light of a fluid culture is another. Knowledge, plus intuition, is the way to lead and manage.

Which way are you looking?

Reflection: Evaluate your teams; make a list of the most valuable players—both paid and unpaid leaders. Once you have this list, rate them from one to ten, with one being the absolute best person who needs no supervision and ten being a person who needs a lot of supervision. Start reconfiguring your staff so that most of them are between one and three. You do not have the luxury to spend your time with the others, no matter how much you might like them.

The Effect of Radical Change on Organizations

L iving at such a unique time of historical transition means we must change everything, including how we organize. In order to survive in today's world, organizations have to be able to quickly adapt to the new environment. That means major change.

No one organizational style will work from church to church. The shape of the organization will vary depending on the vision and the surrounding environment. That means we need to develop new ways to look at local church organizations.

Established organizations often find it hardest to reorganize in times of significant change. They may have done well until now, so they are blinded to the changes around them and find it doubly hard to see old things in new ways.

Consider mainline Protestantism and the Roman Catholic Church. For two hundred years, they dominated the religious landscape in the United States. Now both are in disarray, primarily because they ignored the recent cultural transitions. Their success blinded them to the changes all around them. Let's dig deeper and single out two denominations that are in free fall due to their inability to change.

The United Methodist Church was a success because of its itinerant system, deploying pastors from church to church by horseback. The Lutheran Church was a success because it gave immigrants coming from Europe a spiritual home away from home. Today, both denominations are in rapid decline. For the United Methodist Church, we believe this is largely because it insists on moving its pastors from church to church even though the move is not necessary or prudent for the church. For the Lutheran Church, it is because the boats don't come from Europe anymore.

The United Methodist itinerant system worked because the people settled in one place while the circuit riders rode from place to place. The itinerant preacher was only a method of carrying out the vision. It wasn't the vision. Over time, however, it became ingrained as the vision even though it hasn't worked since World War II.

The Lutheran Church is ready if more Europeans with a Lutheran background should arrive. Because it was primed for churched immigrants, the Lutheran Church now finds it difficult to gain a passion for evangelism and reach out to the unchurched people in their own backyards.

Both denominations were so successful that they were blinded to the radical changes going on around them, and thus they have been unable to adjust and be effective in today's world.

Church as an Organic Metaphor

Before the fourth transition, organizations were looked upon as machines. All one had to do was fix it. Tweaking was mostly the name of the game. Order, stability, and predictability were the goals. Most churches are still structured like machines.

But now organizations have become organic and unpredictable. They don't move forward in a straight line. There are unforeseen consequences about which no one can plan. That uncertainty leads to fear.

Fear has a way of taking the EQ out of the picture and stifling innovation. That is why the effective leader has to relish radical change. If you're afraid of risk, you probably won't do well in the new world.

Let's consider an organic metaphor, looking at organizations as living beings.[1] Just as the human species has to adapt to a changing environment for survival, organizations have to adapt in order to survive and, hopefully, thrive.

The organic metaphor is at the heart of what is wrong with established denominations. They function like machines where one model of governance is imposed on every church regardless of the situation. That's one of the reasons independent churches are often better positioned for success in our current cultural environment.

For denominational churches, the temptation is to try to turn around their decline by tweaking the existing systems rather than thinking from a fresh perspective. Recall the biblical issue of putting new wine in old wineskins?

I (SM) had an experience of this with the church where I am a pastor. As I have said, we have done a lot of experimenting. Ultimately, that meant we made organizational changes, which required a new constitution. Our judicatory leaders were very helpful and encouraging. But the biggest problem was that our denominational model constitution demands that the governing board be called a church council.

We wanted it to be a smaller group called a vision team—to lessen the notion of a controlling board and focus clearly on the task of vision alone. Our constitution now says that we have a church council, but our bylaws state that in our church we are going to call the council a vision team.

The point is that this task took far too much time, compromise, and effort. Why is it deemed necessary for my denomination to have all its boards called councils? What are the implications of this for far greater issues that deal with how we understand what it means to be a church in general and address the dramatic needs of our day?

The organic metaphor forces us to focus on adaptation, learning, and transformation as opposed to revitalization and restructuring. We are way beyond the ability to survive by simply tweaking.[2]

Reflection: Which metaphor best describes your church—machine or organic?

Learning Organizations Are Critical

Using the organic metaphor again, organizations have a human-like living, breathing quality that has to morph with the environment. As we move from one transition to another, the bottom line for an organization is this—those that thrive will be learning organizations.

Although there is a lot of disagreement on the definition of a learning organization, we will use Peter Senge's:

Learning organizations [are] organizations where people continually expand their capacity to create the results they truly desire, where new and expansive patterns of thinking are nurtured, where collective aspiration is set free, and where people are continually learning to see the whole together.[3]

Living things are always growing and adapting. The same is true for successful organizations. They must be constantly learning if they want to thrive in times of great transition. In fact, learning is at the heart of an effective organization. In uncertain times, when all we know for sure is that nothing is for sure, we need organizations that are able to constantly renew and reinvent themselves. Without the habit of learning, the vision will never be executed.

It is for this reason that learning organizations honor their mistakes, learn from them, and do not try to hide them. They will make mistakes and learn from them before others even notice the issue. They will continually defy conventional wisdom and will see the need to learn—not as a weakness but as the only way to exist.

Remember EQ trumps IQ? Learning organizations will focus on identifying how to read the signs of the times. As EQ develops, leaders step out and risk looking foolish by saying, "Just because it has worked for us in the past, I'm not sure it will work going forward." In a way, the more we develop our EQ, the less we know and the more passionate we are about what we don't know.

The equation that works best in changing times is research/development x intuition = desired results. People who follow their intuition don't do it in a vacuum. Instead, they are very aware of what is going on around them. They take "what is" and ask "what will be" without any preconceived idea of their final decision.[4]

So what are some general assumptions for learning organizations that rely on data and intuition in times of radical change like we described in chapter 1?

Adaptive Systems Are Essential

Our society and all of its institutions are now in a continuous process of transformation. We must learn to understand, guide, influence, and manage these transformations. We must make the capacity for undertaking them integral to ourselves and to our institutions. As we learn more about the new world and how it might function, we shift the emphasis and structure of our organization. The systems we rely on to grow the church and kingdom will have to change.

Systems are different from strategic plans. Systems are a way of doing things that will cause a person to learn from mistakes. For our purposes, most churches operate in a single site system—one church in one location. That has been the way of doing church for centuries, but it isn't anymore.

An excellent example of an adaptive learning system is the rise of the multisite church. At first, it emerged as an act of desperation as single site churches grew to the point they were out of room, so they experimented with off-site worship. Why did they do this? Because their desire would not let them hang out a "No Vacancy" sign, and their intuition suggested the multisite approach might work. Their desire was based on their calling, and their intuition was based on the data that came out of how the church functioned in New Testament times.

By following this passion and mission, we have seen that multisite churches

- grow faster than church plants
- have more actual first-time believers
- are less expensive
- have more lay participation
- are more effective than adding on to the first campus
- make it easier to reach a different culture or place

Now multisites are so prevalent they may become the norm in a few decades. None of this would happen in a stable, nonlearning organization where "we've never done it that way before" was the culture.

We must become able not only to transform our institutions in response to changing situations and requirements but also invent and develop institutions that are learning systems capable of bringing about their own continual transformation.

An example of such a system is what we did at every staff meeting when I (BE) was a pastor. We examined the progress of every new person who signed in and then assigned someone to check up on them the following week. Our goal was two-fold: (1) to pursue their return and staying, and (2) to learn why they did or didn't. Then we would work on improving the things that we learned weren't working.

Another system was what I called the "Span of Influence." Notice it isn't "span of control." Innovation never happens when an organization is under control. However, there is a need for supervision, coaching, and oversight. The less centralized the decision-making, the more likely a church is to thrive. In a decentralized organization, action can be taken more quickly to solve problems at lower organizational levels, more people provide input into decisions, and employees are less likely to feel alienated. The fewer people reporting to the center, the more likely new ways of carrying out the overall vision will quickly emerge.

I (BE) was consulting with a church several years ago where all the staff people, twenty-four of them, were reporting to the lead pastor. The church was growing, but not nearly as fast as the lead pastor wanted. After spending a week with them, I was able to convince them that a span of influence of four was better than what they were doing. We reduced the span of influence to where no one, including the pastor, had more than four people reporting to him or her. The church exploded with growth over the next two decades. When the lead pastor, or anyone on the staff, has more people than this reporting to them, that person is likely to become a bottleneck for the growth of the church.

When you keep the span of influence to four, especially for the lead pastor, he or she has the time to envision and strategize about the future. In addition, staff members are now required to grow their leadership skills as they learn to supervise as well.

The more a church uses this system

- the less likely any one person is to become a bottleneck;
- the more likely innovation is to occur;
- the more likely staff will grow their leadership skills in their area of ministry.

Reflection: Describe your organizational structure. How adept is your church at learning from what is going on around it and making middle-of-the-road changes in rapid fashion?

Decentralization Is Fundamental

Rapid change requires decentralized organizations. The world of the top-down, command- and control-center type of leadership is quickly going away. In its place is a decentralized, self-organizing, self-starting, team-based, collaborative structure. The less supervision needed, without abdicating authority, the better. When the vision is embedded throughout the organization, there is little need for top-down control. In place of control, staff members need living role models of effectiveness.

In such an organization, diversity is valued over homogeneity; flexible networks are valued over silo-type departments; mission statements replace job descriptions; and clear expectations replace heavy-handed rules and surveillance.

Unlike the machine-oriented organization with boxes and factory lines, organic organizations are seen as a collection of complementary and interrelated subsystems bound together by a vision (see these two realities depicted in the images below). Just as the brain delegates cognitive matters to different parts of itself, so the organic organization diffuses decision making throughout the staff. It can do this only because the vision is sufficiently embedded in every staff person.

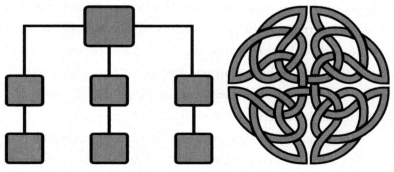

Previously, the business world spoke of *formalization*. Formalization refers to the degree to which jobs within the organization are standardized. A highly formalized job gives the person a minimum amount of discretion over what is to be done, when it is to be done, and how he or she should do it. Employees can be expected to handle the same input in exactly the same way all the time.

In today's world, we are finding "low formalization" to be more effective. In low formalization, job behaviors are relatively unprogrammed and employees have a great deal of freedom to exercise discretion in their work.

Compare this to job descriptions in churches. Most of them confine the staff to certain tasks or areas of ministry. When people are hired to fulfill a job description in a world that is radically changing, it is not uncommon to hear, "That's not in my job description." In the world we are moving into, job descriptions will curtail both the growth of a church and staff. It's better to hire based on joining a journey with an undetermined destination. If you are going to have job descriptions, then always put in the clause "and anything else the goals require."

When I (BE) hired someone, I asked the person to share with me his or her spiritual journey, and then I showed that person our mission statement. If the person resonated with it, I told them to go home and write their job description in a way that would fulfill the vision. When they returned, if what they presented seemed appropriate to the vision, they were hired with one caveat—everything in the job description may change as the church developed.

When you hire this way, two important things take place: (1) the new staff person has bought into and understands the vision, and (2) the new staff person has had major input into how he or she will fulfill their part of the vision.

Embrace Disequilibrium

In times of epic change, organizations must be willing to abandon familiar organizational behaviors and principles, learning to embrace disequilibrium. That's right, embrace disequilibrium. Stability and the status quo are disastrous for organizations as we enter the fourth and possibly the fifth great transition.

Organizations change in direct proportion to their dissatisfaction with the status quo. For that reason, in changing times it is essential to keep an organization stirred up with a measure of discontent regarding the way things are. Ministry-as-usual is the main enemy in times of great change. Ministry-as-usual is not a safe harbor from the storms of disruption; it is a dead end. In other words, the cost of the status quo is greater than the risk of major change.

About seven years ago, I (SM) ran out of vision for our church. That had never been a problem before. It was most distressing. We are a church of never-ending discontent. We always want to connect one more person to Jesus, but I didn't have the sense of what was next to help make that happen.

So I decided to check out what Bill Easum was doing. I discovered that he had a partner, Bill Tenny-Brittian, who had recently moved to within only thirty miles from me. That seemed like a rather clear word from God.

There was some threat in this, however. What would Bill Tenny-Brittian think of me? What would he think of our church?

Again, this was a bumpy journey. Some people left. I had a health problem. I told a couple staff people they no longer had a job. We did a renovation that ended up costing far more than the estimates. I dramatically changed how I understood myself as a pastor. We changed the organization of the church in revolutionary ways.

We now may just be the most hospitable church in town—not because I say so, but because our first-time guests say so. Our church is far more aligned with God's desires today than it was seven years ago. I celebrate our holy journey through disequilibrium.

Tweaking Is Senseless

Never tweak a strategy or program just to keep the status quo afloat. Doing so dulls the organization to the changes going on around it and makes it content with or resigned to the way things are. Nothing could be worse in times of major transition. When an organization is content, it is less likely to realize what is taking place around it. It is reluctant to experiment, thus making adaptation impossible. The emperor needs to know he has no clothes and one of the primary roles of a leader is to define the reality facing the organization. So being out of equilibrium is the prelude to both understanding and adapting to the changing environment.

A good example of how disequilibrium helps foster adaptation is seen in the way pilots are trained. One of the exercises student pilots have is to go "under the hood," which allows the instructor to try to disorientate them by turning the plane up-down-and-around before handing the stick to the student, who quickly has to change everything to get the plane back on level. The student has to figure out where the horizon is, reorient the plane, and return to being on course.

Many pastors, churches, and denominations continue to struggle to keep the status quo. Instead of throwing everything out and starting over, they are trying to build on a faulty way of organizing and leading that no longer works. Like the student pilot who freezes instead of making the necessary changes, the church crashes and burns.

Case in point: not long ago we worked with a denomination that experienced a split over a social issue. Enough of their tribe left the denomination that they decided to plant a number of new churches. But instead of starting from scratch, they kept the same leadership, structure, and way of doing business (even though they said they didn't). They tried to tweak the status quo just a bit, hoping for a different outcome. Care to guess what happened?

Let's not kid ourselves—change for the sake of change results in failure. It's one thing to make a major change based on solid intuition; it's another to fall victim to inconsistency. If you are going to instigate disequilibrium, you must remain focused on your practices, expectations, and priorities. Like the pilot, you must figure out how to discover the desired course.

Staff Is an Investment Not a Cost

In the Modern Age, employees were considered a cost. Organizations considered the cost ratio between the number of workers and profit. Unfortunately, too many church leaders still consider staff to be a necessary cost of doing ministry with the goal being to have as few staff people as possible.

Today, effective organizations realize that their employees are their greatest assets. They invest in their growth by providing lifetime learning experiences. While the Modern Age invested in machines, now the world has begun investing more time, energy, and money in people. Churches ought to do the same. Wise churches set aside money for each staff person to be able to attend conferences, hire a coach, or whatever will grow their potential.

So instead of thinking cost ratio, the effective church considers the relational ratio when evaluating how much they are spending on staff. Relational ratio suggests that the purpose of staff isn't to generate programs but to grow people. The more effective a church staff is, both paid and unpaid, the more relationships are established, and the more likely people are to be retained long enough to be apprenticed into a disciple.

Collective Collaboration Results in Innovation

When a group of people are involved in a project with the freedom to act on their own, there is a good possibility of innovation happening. Some call this the "hive mind."[5]

The concept comes from the way bees function when they move. Bees swarm in unison as if guided by some overriding passion. Effective teamwork is like a swarm of bees moving together, seemingly one mind and body.

Innovation occurs when: (1) the primary controlling factor is the vision, not a board; (2) self-organizing, self-governing, and self-dissolving teams are free to experiment; (3) the vision is decentralized and adaptation is fostered; and (4) effective teamwork is in place.

Let us digress for a moment and say that line-item budgets are a great way to kill initiative and innovation. If you look at most churches, you will find a budget that spells out how to spend the money item by item. If and when one of the line items is overspent, leaders get unhappy. This method worked in a predictable world. But we no longer live in such a world. A church doesn't know from one month to another what it will need to do, much less year by year.

The best method is to decide what is needed at the moment to make the vision happen, and then set out to find the funds. Even if a church does an annual budget drive, it shouldn't allocate the money to line items. Money should be kept in a big, liquid pool with one exception—a mortgage payment, if the church has one. Even money for staff should not be considered a fixed item. Salary should be up for grabs every year depending on a person's effectiveness. That way, as the money is needed, it can be used without jumping through hoops.

The Smaller the Organization the Quicker the Adaptation

The larger an organization, the harder it is to turn it around or to make major decisions. The smaller the organization, the easier it is to turn it around or make major decisions. So it makes sense to keep the organization small in changing times.

The best example of an effective organization is a mom-and-pop store. Mom and pop can make rapid major decisions while eating dinner or lying in bed. But then consider an organization like the church that has to go through several committees and then a board in order to make a major decision. Or a denomination that meets only once every four years to make major decisions. In such cases, decision-making takes forever. Notice the missing word—*rapid*. Large organizations simply can't make rapid decisions unless the board gives the CEO the power to do so. You seldom see that freedom to act in a congregation. That's why in times of great change, church boards should be kept under seven people. Three people would be better, with none of them members of the church except the lead pastor. That's also why effective churches don't need any standing committees. All that is needed is a board that sets policy, holds the pastor accountable, and gets out of the way.

Reflection: What is the size of your board? What authority does it have? Can it make a million dollar decision in one meeting?

Moving toward the Edge of Chaos

In times of major change, organizations need to move toward the edge of chaos. They need to feed off innovation and experimentation. They can't be afraid of making a mistake. They must to be willing to go down paths not yet traveled and explore ideas and solutions that have never been tried. When that happens, the bulk of people experience confusion and a feeling of chaos. If your church isn't feeling this confusion, you're still trying to live out the status quo. You're stuck in an age that no longer exists.

A biblical example of this is when the Israelites left Egypt for Canaan. You would think anything would be better than making bricks out of mud. But as soon as the celebration of freedom wore off, confusion and chaos reared their ugly heads. The people complained, as we see in Exodus 14:11, "Weren't there enough graves in Egypt that you took us away to die in the desert?"

The "finding life at the edge of chaos" concept is difficult for established churches with a long-standing tradition in the way things are done. For some leaders, it is almost heresy to talk about changing. In a relatively slow-moving world like the one we've transitioned from, the church could pride itself on being a bulwark of stability, but not so any more. Remember the chart? The rate of change has escalated. Again, let that resonate. Has your church changed as much in the past decade or two as our culture has?

The Core Vision

Examine the effective churches in the world and you will see that most of them emerged out of a single person's vision who had the self-confidence to empower others to execute that vision. Effective organizations do not just happen. They emerge out of the cauldron of a burning, passionate vision.

So the question you must ask is, "How on fire am I?" The quote frequently attributed to John Wesley is still at the heart of it all. When people asked him why so many came to hear him preach, he said, "I set myself on fire and people come to watch me burn." That's the kind of passion from which great organizations and movements emerge.

New Shapes and Forms Are Commonplace

When living organisms adapt to the environment, they self-organize, allowing new forms and shapes to emerge out of the chaos. Here are several examples of how organizations and innovations morphed in times of great change.

One example of this adaptation was the Protestant Reformation. No one had any idea where the church was going or if there even would be a church because of all the splintering. But new groups emerged to form a different type of church. The same thing is happening today.

Another example was the way Dee Hock organized VISA. He saw the coming revolution in technology and the Internet. So he started a virtual organization with no standing office or location—just accounts in banks.[6]

The primary things by which we will soon live our lives haven't even been dreamed of yet. Some leaders will execute their dreams and make them reality and all of us will be changed by it.

Embedding the Vision Is the Ultimate Goal

As we saw in the chart in chapter 1, throughout most of history, change has been a series of evolutionary and incremental changes interrupted by a radical discontinuity between one age and the next. We clearly seem to be living in one of those periods of radical discontinuity. In such times, evolutionary and incremental changes are senseless.

Today, if an organization is to succeed, an adaptive spirit has to be embedded in the system itself. The organization must become so radically disconnected with the past that it's open to all possibilities. Or to put it in spiritual terms, it is open to the unpredictable moving of the Holy Spirit. With no shackles to the past, it is free to follow the Spirit wherever it leads. Such freedom requires an awesome vision of the future and confidence in God's leadership. Surely we learned that from the Gospels and the book of Revelation. All things are moving forward to the climax—the rule of God over everything and everyone.

In the meantime, we find ourselves left with a world in transition. Like a monk looking at his first hardbound book or today's ninety-year-old using a computer for the first time, we are staring at a new, unfamiliar world. This new world requires different skills, but more importantly, it requires an inquiring mind that is open to anything that revolves around the God-given vision left for us by Jesus—"Go make disciples."

Chapter Five
Seize the Moment

T urning vision into reality will be quite a feat in a time like ours. We can't go about ministry as if it is 1950 or 1975 or even 2000. Those dates are long past. Our cultural changes are speeding through history at an escalating rate, the likes of which humankind has never experienced before.

For our churches to thrive, they must be willing to change how they think and do things, even if they are thriving at the moment. Pastors will have to learn new skills and see what isn't yet seen, trying new ways for communicating the good news, even if they don't like it. New expectations will need to be clearly communicated and staff held accountable to those expectations. Organizations must learn how to execute on the fly without being burdened by rules and regulations. Instead of thinking our way into the future, we will have to act our way into new forms of thinking.

Most churches will have trouble with all this change. They will try to stabilize their systems, tweak their structure, and continue to believe that things will get back to normal in time.

Our hope is that you are now able to understand the need to see old things in new ways and are willing to take major leaps of faith into the new transition. The more adventurous you are by nature, the more you will enjoy the ride. We applaud those who are willing to stick their necks out and try new, crazy things for the Gospel.

Pastors, this is your opportunity to seize the moment. Learn from the lessons of the past. Grab hold of God's desired future for you, your congregation, and the church as a whole. We would love to hear your comments on the concepts of the book and enter into conversation with you. Again, you can e-mail us at: http://effectivechurch.com/contact/.

As you go forward, remember the promise Jesus made to us in Matthew 28:20: "I myself will be with you every day until the end of this present age." What more do we need?

For Further Reading

In writing this book, we are indebted to several authors whose thoughts you will find sprinkled throughout the pages. We have taken many of their ideas, blended them with our experiences, and formulated a way for pastors to be more effective in turning visions into reality. They are:

Bennis, Warren G., and Patricia Ward Biederman. *Organizing Genius: The Secrets of Creative Collaboration.* Reading, MA: Addison-Wesley, 1997.

Bossidy, Larry, and Ram Charan. *Execution: The Discipline of Getting Things Done.* New York: Crown Business, 2002.

Charan, Ram, and Stephen J. Drotter. *The Leadership Pipeline: How to Build the Leadership-Powered Company.* San Francisco: Jossey-Bass, 2001.

Crouch, Andy. *Playing God: Redeeming the Gift of Power.* Downers Grove, IL: InterVarsity Press, 2013.

Goleman, Daniel, and Richard E. Boyatzis. *Primal Leadership: Realizing the Power of Emotional Intelligence.* Boston: Harvard Business School Press, 2002.

Heifetz, Ronald A. *Leadership without Easy Answers.* Cambridge, MA: Belknap Press of Harvard University Press, 1994.

Hill, Linda A., and Kent Lineback. *Being the Boss: The 3 Imperatives for Becoming a Great Leader.* Boston: Harvard Business Review Press, 2011.

Hirschhorn, Larry. *Reworking Authority Leading and Following in the Post-Modern Organization.* Cambridge, MA: MIT Press, 1998.

Hock, Dee. *Birth of the Chaordic Age.* San Francisco: Berrett-Koehler Publishers, 1999.

Imparato, Nicholas and Oren Harari. *Jumping the Curve: Innovation and Strategic Choice in an Age of Transition.* San Francisco: Jossey-Bass, 1994.

Kelly, Kevin. *Out of Control: The Rise of Neo-Biological Civilization.* Reading, MA: Addison-Wesley, 1994.

Kotter, John P. *Leading Change.* Boston: Harvard Business School Press, 1996.

Mohler, R. Albert. *The Conviction to Lead: 25 Principles for Leadership That Matters.* Minneapolis: Bethany House, 2012.

Morgan, Gareth. *Images of Organization: The Executive Edition.* Thousand Oaks, CA: Sage Publications, 1998.

Pascale, Richard T., and Mark Millemann. *Surfing the Edge of Chaos: The Laws of Nature and the New Laws of Business.* New York: Crown Business, 2000.

Ramo, Joshua Cooper. *The Age of the Unthinkable: Why the New World Disorder Constantly Surprises Us and What to Do about It.* New York: Little, Brown and Company, 2009.

Rogers, Everett M. *Diffusion of Innovations.* 3rd ed. New York: Free Press, 1983.

Schlesinger, Leonard A., and Charles F. Kiefer. *Just Start: Take Action, Embrace Uncertainty, Create the Future.* Boston: Harvard Business Review Press, 2012.

Notes

Introduction

1. Bill Easum, *Unfreezing Moves: Following Jesus into the Mission Field* (Nashville: Abingdon Press, 2001).

2. Bill Easum, *Leadership on the Other Side: No Rules, Just Clues* (Nashville: Abingdon Press, 2000).

1. The Key to Everything

1. Bill Easum, *Dancing with Dinosaurs: Ministry in a Hostile and Hurting World* (Nashville: Abingdon Press, 1993), 23–36.

2. "Billionaires on a Mission: Titans at the Table," *Bloomberg*, online video, 21:57, January 23, 2014, accessed April 16, 2016, http://www.bloomberg.com/news/videos/b/34b7d289-cb23 -413f-b0a5-1546eea3dae8.

3. Bill Easum and Bill Tenny-Brittian, *Doing Ministry in Hard Times* (Nashville: Abingdon Press, 2010).

4. Nicholas Imparato and Oren Harari, *Jumping the Curve: Innovation and Strategic Choice in an Age of Transition* (San Francisco: Jossey-Bass, 1994).

5. Bob Dylan, "The Times They Are a-Changin'," recorded October 24, 1963, on *The Times They Are a-Changin'* album, Columbia, 1964.

6. *"Did You Know 3.0"* (Officially updated for 2012) HD,

YouTube video, 4:58, posted by VideoShredHead, February 28, 2012, https://www.youtube.com/watch?v=YmwwrGV_aiE.

2. The Art of Execution

1. S.M.A.R.T. goals first appeared in a November 1981 issue of *Management Review* (vol. 70, issue 11), in an article titled "There's a S.M.A.R.T. way to write management's goals and objectives," by George Doran, Arthur Miller, and James Cunningham.

2. Bill Easum and Bill Tenny-Brittian, *Effective Staffing for Vital Churches: The Essential Guide to Finding and Keeping the Right People* (Grand Rapids, MI: Baker Books, 2012).

3. From tour notes taken by Bill Easum in Canada in 2000.

4. Ron Ashkenas, Dave Ulrich, Todd Jick and Steve Kerr, Steve, *The Boundaryless Organization: Breaking the Chains of Organizational Structure* (San Francisco: Jossey-Bass, 2002).

3. The Role of the Leader in Execution

1. Daniel Goleman, Richard Boyatzis, and Annie McKee, *Primal Leadership: Realizing the Power of Emotional Intelligence,* (Boston: Harvard Business School Press, 2002), 247–50.

2. "Active Learning," Center for Research on Learning and Teaching, accessed April 29, 2015, http://www.crlt.umich.edu/tstrategies/tsal.

3. Larry Hirschhorn, *Reworking Authority: Leading and Following in the Post-Modern Organization,* (Cambridge, MA: MIT Press, 1998).

4. Andy Crouch, *Playing God: Redeeming the Gift of Power* (Downers Grove, IL: InterVarsity Press, 2013), 13.

5. Rob Lebow and Randy Spitzer, *Accountability: Freedom and Responsibility without Control* (San Francisco: Berrett-Koehler, 2002), 7.

6. Bill Easum, *Sacred Cows Make Gourmet Burgers: Ministry Anytime, Anywhere, by Anybody* (Nashville: Abingdon Press, 1995).

7. From an interview conducted by Bill Easum at the Church of the Resurrection in 2000.

8. Price Waterhouse Team, *The Paradox Principles: How High-Performance Companies Manage Chaos, Complexity, and Contradiction to Achieve Superior Results* (Chicago: Irwin Professional Pub, 1995).

4. The Effect of Radical Change on Organizations

1. For a description of eight metaphors for the postmodern organizational life, see Gareth Morgan, *Images of Organization: The Executive Edition* (Thousand Oaks, CA: Sage Publications, 1998).

2. For more on why revitalization won't work today, see Bill Easum, *A Second Resurrection: Leading Your Congregation to New Life* (Nashville: Abingdon Press, 2007).

3. Peter Senge, *The Fifth Discipline: The Art and Practice of the Learning Organization* (New York: Doubleday/Currency, 1990), 3.

4. Sarita Chawla and John Renesch, *Learning Organizations: Developing Cultures for Tomorrow's Workplace* (Portland, OR: Productivity Press, 1995). This is an anthology of essays from thirty-nine of the leading voices on organizational life. Church leaders wanting to reshape the culture of their church will find this book helpful. Church leaders ready to give up control and bureaucracy and move to an organic form of congregational life will find this book a useful tool.

5. Kevin Kelly, *Out of Control: The New Biology of Machines, Social Systems and the Economic World* (Reading, MA: Addison-Wesley, 1995), 5–28.

6. Dee Hock, *Birth of the Chaordic Age* (San Francisco: Berrett-Koehler Publishers, 1999).

CPSIA information can be obtained
at www.ICGtesting.com
Printed in the USA
LVOW01s0357210816
501118LV00003B/3/P